This edition first published in the UK by Fairfield Books Ltd 2020

© Fairfield Books Ltd 2020

ISBN: 978-1-909811-57-7

Editors: Phil Walker, Jo Harman, Matt Thacker

Design: Joe Provis
Photographs: Getty Images

Print: Jellyfish Print Solutions

Acknowledgements
The publishers would like to thank all of the contributors and
Eleanor Oldroyd for providing the photo for her essay.

GOLDEN SUMMERS

fairfield books

CONTENTS

1934	Robert Winder	Pageantry between the wars	12
1945	James Holland	Emerging from the wreckage	15
1947	Henry Blofeld	My local boy and the great god of batting	18
1948	Stephen Fay	Bradman's Invincibles	20
1949	Rod Edmond	Walter Hadlee and his Kiwi companions	23
1954/55	David Frith	'Typhoon' Tyson and the blow to the head that changed everything	26
1960	Ted Dexter	Coming out swinging	30
1964	Stephen Brenkley	Being Kenny	33
1966	Stephen Chalke	Sobers takes centre stage	36
1967	Christopher Sandford	The velvet gloves of JT Murray	39
1967/68	Suresh Menon	India's awakening	42
1975	Paul Edwards	Wind of change	45
1976	Vic Marks	The long, hot summer of Viv and 'Cappy'	48
1976/77	Ashley Gray	The Australian civil war	51
1977	Jon Hotten	The return of the bespectacled mutineer	54
1978	Pat Murphy	Access all areas at Edgbaston	57
1979	Matt Thacker	Sunday remembrances	61
1981	Tom Holland	In the court of Sir Ian	64
1982	Andy Zaltzman	All-rounders of the Cricketpocalypse	67
1983	Simon Barnes	The year of the underdog	70
1984	Tanya Aldred	The maroon-blazered galácticos	73
1985	Daniel Norcross	Lessons in love	78
1986/87	Anthony McGowan	Two trials down under	82
1987	Eleanor Oldroyd	A woman in a man's world	86
1989	Andrew Miller	The warm blanket of defeat	89
1990	Lawrence Booth	Love, loss and Allan Lamb	92
1991	Derek Pringle	A regal summer	95
1992/93	Firdose Moonda	Conflicts of allegiance	98
1993	Phil Walker	Run-outs, break-ups and well-meaning cluelessness	101
1993/94	Sam Perry	Australia's game catches fire	104
1994	Emma John	Bad things happen to good people	107
1994/95	Adam Collins	Australia call in the A-team	110
1995	Ross Armstrong	Theatres of dreams	113
1997	Jo Harman	New hope, New Labour and Ben Hollioake	116

1997/98	**John Stern**	Youth and young manhood	120
1998	**Vithushan Ehantharajah**	Murali makes Sri Lankan voices heard	124
1999	**Felix White**	Chasing down edges like it's 1999	127
2000	**Alan Gardner**	New millennium, new England	130
2000/01	**Geoff Lemon**	The field is set	134
2002	**Henry Cowen**	Building shrines to life's triers	137
2003	**Ed Kemp**	The blue-aired din of adult battle	140
2004	**Paul Ford**	The sweet taste of defeat	143
2005	**Tim Key**	The big one	146
2008	**Dean Wilson**	The man who fell to Earth	149
2009	**Isabelle Westbury**	Stepping into the void	152
2014	**Andrew Fidel Fernando**	The eight-month party	156
2014/15	**Melinda Farrell**	Out of the darkness and into the light	159
2017	**Heather Knight**	The day everything changed	162
2019	**Mark Wood**	Across the universe	166
2020	**Scyld Berry**	The season unlike any other	170

INTRODUCTION

Inside these pages are contained 50 essays from as many different writers, covering a half-century of distinct yet inseparable cricketing years.

You'll find here every conceivable style of cricket writing, a cornucopia of actors, musicians, comedians, historians and even a couple of World Cup winners muscling in alongside some of the finest cricket writers in the game. It makes on paper for a formidable cast list, and quite a show. A galaxy of stars, if you will, and usefully affordable ones at that.

Very few arms needed twisting. Almost everyone who was asked to contribute was up for it, and I guess it stands to reason: who wouldn't, given the luxuriant licence of the first-person, fancy having a run at articulating, at *getting to the bottom of*, this evidently irrational, defiantly persistent fixation with balls and bats and floppy hats. The chance for a cricket lover to delve into how they ended up where they are, arranging the moments that shaped that love around the big stuff of the day, is not easily resisted.

Cricket, they say, is just escapism. It's a day off, a departure, a sublime waste of time that matters only because it doesn't. And there is, and has to be, some truth in that – it is just a game in the end, albeit *the* game. In these pages you'll find a handful of writers wrestling with this point, but no more than a few. More likely you'll be struck by the game's gravitational force, the feeling of being pulled towards something, offering a way *in*, not a way out. It's the first match we saw. It's the catch we dropped in the rain. It's the moment we fell in love. It is history, family, identity, memory. It seems to me that this is cricket's real genius: It can be as little or as much as we allow it to be.

So maybe it's not so irrational after all. Who's to say that such devotion doesn't offer a pretty sensible response to the rootlessness of the real? That this way of life is any less plausible than another? After all, one doesn't merely *like* cricket. It's not really a game that can be taken or left. It remains either impenetrable or inescapable.

Each writer took the gig on their own terms. The brief was deliberately loose. Some kept their voice relatively muted and majored on the cricket taking place at the time. A few took themselves out of the story completely and let the game speak for itself. Others sidled along towards confessional memoir to see what that might throw up; most took bits from some or all of the above.

Memory keeps cropping up, in some cases as a kind of nagging concern that the recalled stories of our past are impressions of the real facts, and therefore flimsy. It's against this fuzziness where those irrefutable dots and digits come in. Cricket people, you will recognise, possess a strange capacity to measure their lives against the Test match duels and tournament failures of the day. When I came to revisit the moments of 1993 for my own entry – Atherton's run out, Warne's first ball, Suchy's debut – it felt like flicking through the pages of a dusty old diary, pulling those parched scorecards down off the shelf, for the stories to spill out from there.

This book is about famous moments from cricket's greatest years. But it's also about that other place, beyond the primly cut squares of ascertainable fact, among the rolling outfields of personal experience. Among the outer reaches, where cricket lives and breathes. Where the *real* stuff happens.

Phil Walker, November 2020

ROBERT WINDER

1934

PAGEANTRY BETWEEN THE WARS

An historic Hedley Verity-inspired victory at Lord's was just the start of an amazing sporting spectacle that lit up the summer of 1934

When Graeme Swann sealed a rare Ashes win at Lord's in 2009 (bowling Mitchell Johnson) the celebration was given extra warmth by the fact that this was the first English victory in this famous fixture for over 70 years. But flicking back to that grand day in 1934, when Australia were toppled by the left-arm spin of Yorkshire's Hedley Verity, I was surprised to learn that this was not merely the last time England had beaten Australia at Lord's: it was the only time they won there in the entire 20th century. And it was the high point of an unusually tense summer, since this was the rematch following the furious winter of 1932/33, when Douglas Jardine's England had battered Bradman and company in Adelaide and Sydney, using Harold Larwood's electrifying bowling as the spearhead of a bad-tempered new gambit: Bodyline.

So the atmosphere at Lord's that grey weekend was rapt with expectation.

England batted first and scored 440, and when Verity dismissed the Don in the first innings (caught and bowled, following a strangely hesitant swish) the billboards read simply: "He's out!" Bradman was a *nonpareil*, so everyone knew what that meant.

Australia finished the second day on 192-2, leaving the game well-balanced. But overnight rain gave the next day's pitch a dark green tinge, and when Verity looked out of his hotel window he could see gleams of water streaking silver on the road.

"I shouldn't wonder if we don't have a bit of fun today," he murmured.

When he came on to bowl a few hours later, drifting to the wicket in that famously unhurried way of his – "lightly and decisively", as his captain put it – the game at once took on a fresh complexion. As always, Verity found "an impeccable length" right away, but the ball was turning and lifting too. In the

Crowds queue
up for the
second Ashes
Test at Lord's

slips, Walter Hammond was smiling. "We knew," he said later, "that the Lord had delivered them into our hands."

It didn't take long. Out they marched, the baggy green caps, and back they traipsed. As Herbert Sutcliffe put it: "When the rain had done his work, Verity was able to do *his* work, and that was the end of it." He took 6-37 in a flash, and when Australia followed on he was at it again, plucking their feathers like a fox in a chicken coop.

As always, the key wicket was Bradman's. From the word go he seemed fidgety, and when Verity floated one at his leg stump he leapt at it, dropped his shoulder like a novice and had a swing. The ball flashed high into the murky Lord's air until Ames trotted forward and took the catch. Australia's chief and legendary hope was gone.

In Bill Bowes' view it was "one of the worst shots he ever played"; Bob Wyatt judged it born of "desperation". Either way, the heart seemed to go out of Australia in a rush. They came, they took guard, and back they went. The last wicket fell at 10 to six, meaning that Verity had bowled virtually unchanged for over five hours, taking 14 wickets in a single day – bettering his merely useful 7-61 in the first innings with a superlative 8-43 in the second. After tea he snagged six for just 15 runs.

Verity's stunning effort was only the start of the amazing sporting pageant that lit up the summer of 1934. On the same day he polished off the Australians, Henry Cotton was setting out on what would prove to be a record-breaking tilt for the Claret Jug at Royal St George's in Kent (the historic 65 he shot in the first round actually inspired Dunlop to name a golf ball after it). And a week or so later, a coming thing named Frederick Perry was warming up for the first of his three Wimbledon victories.

There had not been a home champion in either of these great events for years (Arthur Gore was the last English winner of Wimbledon in 1909, and Jim Barnes' Open win in 1925 was only a memory) just as there had been no victory over Australia at Lord's since 1896. Thanks to the supremacy of American golfers and French tennis stars, the prospect of a domestic triumph in any of these fields seemed remote. But that is what happened in this midsummer rush of 1934. The Lord's Test, the Open, Wimbledon – the three crowning glories of English sport all fell in a single wonderful swoop. It was, to use an overworked term, a shining *annus mirabilis* for English ball games.

There were black clouds behind these silver linings, however. Something profound had perished in the bloody mud of Flanders. No one could forget the way the papers described the lethal first day of the Somme, when 30,000 young men were massacred in just one hour after being ordered to walk – on no account run; vital to keep in formation – into the hot spray of machine gun fire. And then came the General Strike and the Wall Street crash; and the pound was shaken loose from its moorings. Mass unemployment stalked the land, and it was hard to be optimistic about anything.

In 1934 Britain was only just beginning to emerge, dazed and blinking, from all this. Out in the wider world, meanwhile, the silhouettes of new demons – Hitler, Stalin, Mao, Imperial Japan – were darkening the sky. It began to dawn on people that it might be only half-time in the struggle with Germany. The papers were heavy with martial images: naval exercises in Scapa Flow, icy waves crashing over grey decks and forward guns; submarines on the slipway in Barrow-in-Furness; *HMS Malaya* blasting its guns off Spithead, *HMS Sussex* and *HMS Revenge* tooting past Gibraltar.

In the House of Commons the chancellor of the exchequer, Neville Chamberlain, didn't talk about the "long-term economic plan", but turned to Dickens to support his point that the skies were clearing: "We have finished the story of *Bleak House*," he said, "and are sitting down to enjoy the first chapter of *Great Expectations*." It would be silly to suggest that the sporting glories that followed this remark were an actual response to this shift in the national mood, but they certainly came at an opportune time. They suggested that perhaps, maybe, England *could* start enjoying life again.

Not surprisingly, the simple fun of sport was extremely appealing at a time like this. As the *Telegraph* put it, revelling in the "triumph heaping on triumph... success in golf, in tennis, in the cricket field", it was a sign of "recovered national confidence". The *New York Times* made the same point: "It's about time they declared a Bank Holiday over there," it noted, "to celebrate the comeback of Great Britain in sports."

Less than a decade after his historic effort at Lord's, Hedley Verity was hit in the chest by a storm of German bullets as he urged his platoon forward during the 1943 Allied invasion of Sicily. But nothing could erase or dim the memory of the magical afternoon in which he had bewildered and vanquished the mighty Australians. As Neville Cardus, never slow to reach for the most lyrical of moods, put it: "The Gods of the game, who sit up aloft and watch, will remember the loveliness of it all, the style, the poise on light toes, the swing of the arm from noon to evening."

It is possible that in time we will remember Graeme Swann in that sort of way. But then again, maybe not.

Robert Winder was formerly literary editor of the *Independent* and deputy editor of *Granta* magazine. He is the author of *Hell for Leather*, a book about modern cricket.

JAMES HOLLAND

1945

EMERGING FROM THE WRECKAGE

The Victory Tests of 1945 were not merely charged with symbolism; they were rambunctious demonstrations of the wonder of Test match cricket

In the summer of 1945, England played Australia in a series of five Test matches, all of which were charged with a feverish excitement and which, because they were played following the end of the war in Europe and then in the Far East, became known as the Victory Tests. It was not an official series, and there was no urn to be won, but it was hard-fought, watched by packed crowds and, with the exception of a dull draw in the fourth Test, featured some thrilling battles. In fact, it could be argued that the summer of 1945 saw some of the most entertaining Test match cricket ever played.

Cricket had not entirely stopped during the Second World War. The last game in England was Yorkshire against Sussex at Hove, which finished the day Germany marched into Poland on September 1, 1939. The great Hedley Verity took six for almost

nothing, Yorkshire won, and then headed back north. Britain declared war the next day. The following week, he joined up and was later killed fighting in Sicily. He was not the only Test cricketer to give his life, and plenty were wounded or found themselves spending long years as POWs. The majority of first-class cricketers had, however, swapped whites for khaki. This was a world war. Everyone was expected to do their bit – even sporting heroes.

The County Championship had been suspended and so had Test cricket. For spectators, what remained were exhibition matches between the Army and RAF, or Australian Servicemen versus English Servicemen. It was something, and some big names were playing, but it lacked the competitive edge of a first-class game or a Test match.

Somehow, the Victory Tests managed to rekindle that competitive spark despite the lack of official status. They were full of exceptional characters, included a number of both cricketing and war heroes, and they managed to capture the mood perfectly: there was a palpable sense of relief and gratitude, and a celebration of a fabulous game that could be played freely rather than under the looming threat of the swastika. And this extraordinary series, played in a spirit that has rarely, if ever, been bettered by the two great rivals, was to be defined by the emergence of a young Australian cricketer whose free hitting, stunning fielding and ferocious bowling delighted packed crowds. Keith Miller, a fighter pilot in the RAF, demonstrated a devil-may-care *joie de vivre* that has rarely been matched in Ashes Tests. "We were all servicemen," he said, "happy just to be alive and fit and well."

Returning to captain England was Wally Hammond, now 42, and past his prime, but still a colossus of the game. Also included in the team were Len Hutton, Cyril Washbrook and Bill Edrich, all freed from active service. With Verity and Ken Farnes now dead, and with Bill Bowes still recovering from his time as a POW, it was nonetheless a much-depleted side. Nor was there any sign of Denis Compton, who was still serving in the Far East, as was the upcoming batting talent, Reg Simpson.

Australia were without Don Bradman, who managed to duck out of war service with a 'back injury', and were instead dependent on a small handful of Australian soldiers still in Britain – such as their captain, Lindsay Hassett – and a larger proportion of airmen who had been flying with the RAF, many of whom would only ever have this one, golden moment to represent their country, including the spinner Reg Ellis and dashing batsman Ross Stanford. The latter had been the Royal Australian Air Force's leading batsman in 1944 despite flying Lancasters for 617 Dambuster Squadron between matches.

And then there was Miller, who had only just started to make a name for himself back home in Australia when the war had begun. In the summer of 1945, he was still flying Mosquitoes, and in early May, with the war almost over, he had nearly come a cropper during a low-level attack on a German airfield. The aircraft following him was hit and exploded, while Miller had been forced to fly back to base with a napalm tank hanging loosely from his Mosquito's underside.

Just under a week later, the war in Europe was over and Miller was playing in the first Victory Test at Lord's alongside several players who were far from match-fit. One of those was Graham Williams, emaciated after years as a German prisoner of war. When it was his turn to bat, Miller was still at the crease with a hundred under his belt. Emerging through the Long Room and onto the pitch, Williams received a spontaneous and deafening standing ovation. "It was," Miller later recalled, "the most

touching thing I have ever seen or heard, almost orchestral in its sound and feeling. Whenever I think of it, tears still come to my eyes."

The first Test kept the excitement going until the very last ball, after Hammond sped up the over-rate to give the Aussies a sporting chance of victory: 107 runs were needed with 70 minutes remaining on the last day, a target they reached in the final over.

The war was over, the first Victory Test done and dusted, and yet for men like Miller there were still flying duties. On June 28, he was en route to an operation over the Ruhr when his Mosquito suffered engine failure and his starboard motor caught fire. With a wooden wing construction on the Mosquito, this was a potentially fatal disaster, but fortunately the fire extinguisher successfully dampened the flames and he was able to make it back to base in England on one engine. Getting there was one thing, landing was another, and as he touched down the Mosquito bounced, the undercarriage folded, and the aircraft slewed on its belly. A similar crash-landing had killed an Australian squadron leader the week before, but both Miller and his navigator emerged unscathed.

Then it was back to cricket, and four more Tests – at Bramall Lane in Sheffield, at Old Trafford and two more at Lord's. The five-Test series was eventually drawn 2-2, but the extraordinary summer of 'Victory cricket' was not yet over. The season culminated in a Dominions versus England Test at Lord's at the end of August, and was dominated by Miller, who scored a stunning 185 in just 165 minutes. He dispatched the England bowling to all parts, taking 14 off the first over, and hitting the pavilion roof with a six that fell into a hole in the tiles made by shrapnel. There were seven maximums in all. Sir Pelham Warner, former cricketer, president of the MCC and safeguard of the wartime game, declared he had never seen such hitting in his life.

The display struck a chord with all those who watched it. His innings was a *leitmotif* for the moment: the joy of peace, of having survived, of realising that life was to be lived and, above all, enjoyed. That summer, Miller had been asked before one of the Victory Tests about the pressure of playing Test cricket. "I'll tell you what pressure is," he responded. "Pressure is a Messerschmitt up your arse. Cricket is not." Cricket was about entertainment, about sportsmanship. And it was supposed to be fun. No cricketer should ever forget that most important tenet.

James Holland is a historian, author and broadcaster who specialises in the history of the Second World War. He is co-host of the *We Have Ways of Making You Talk* podcast and co-founder of the Chalke Valley History Festival.

A group of men play cricket on a blitzed site in London, set against a backdrop of St Paul's Cathedral

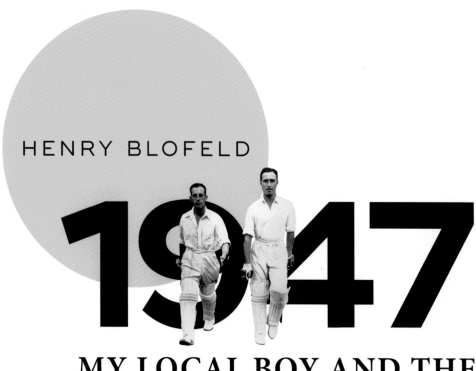

HENRY BLOFELD

1947

MY LOCAL BOY AND THE GREAT GOD OF BATTING

The former Test Match Special *commentator remembers the feats of Denis Compton and Bill Edrich in a sun-drenched summer*

I t was an amazing summer, and the first summer I really got to know about cricket, although I didn't see any of it live. The first time I did was a year later on the third day of the second Test against Australia at Lord's. Instead I listened to it on what was the forerunner of *Test Match Special*. They didn't cover every ball at that stage – that didn't start until '57 and the catalyst was Jim Laker's 19-90 at Old Trafford in '56. The feeling after that was, 'Goodness me, we can't miss these things happening in cricket' and the BBC took that on board. Though not every ball of every Test was on the radio that summer, I certainly remember listening to commentary of Bill Edrich and Denis Compton putting on 370 for the third wicket at Lord's against South Africa.

Edrich and Compton both made a huge number of runs for Middlesex and England that summer. Denis scored 3,816 runs with 18 hundreds and Bill made 3,539 with 12 hundreds, the two highest aggregates made in a summer in England, a record which will never be beaten. It grabbed my attention enormously.

They could hardly have been more different. Denis was tall and extremely good-looking. He was the Brylcreem boy, and he and Keith Miller were the two great icons of cricket during that time. Denis was a very romantic figure, almost fictional, and he was also a unique player – probably the greatest improviser batting has ever known.

Bill was very small, but very competitive. He was more of a man-made player, more workmanlike, but brave as a lion; he flew bombers in the war and won a Distinguished Flying Cross. Denis was in the war too, but he was in India most of the time. Edrich also opened the bowling and bowled fast in a rather uncontrolled way. At Headingley he became only the second player – George Giffen in 1894 was the other – to take four wickets in both innings and make a hundred in the same Test match.

There was never a sense of them competing with each other at all. They couldn't have been more different in style but they complemented one another by their difference.

I knew both well – Bill better than Denis because when he finished at Middlesex he came back and captained Norfolk where I was his vice-captain for seven or eight years. He came from Norfolk, the same as me, and I played village cricket against his family for a lot of my youth, so it was a marriage made in heaven for me.

He was a much more interesting person than Denis Compton. Compton was such a genius he didn't really understand cricket. It seems a strange thing to say but if you asked him about the technique of batting he couldn't really tell you because he had no need to think about it, he did it so naturally.

That was almost the last year Compton was at his absolute peak. He injured his knee playing football very soon after the war and it started to give him trouble. He managed to win the league title with Arsenal the following year, and he had a wonderful season against Australia in '48, but after that the knee really held him back.

Eventually in 1956 he had his right knee-cap removed, and then retuned to make 94 in the final Test of the Ashes. Don Bradman described it as the best innings of the summer. Even after that he played for the Forty Club against Eton, whom I was playing for. He couldn't run in – all he could do was stand and bowl – but he made 30 runs on one leg magnificently. A complete freak was Denis. If he had not got injured, he would have broken every record.

I remember cutting out newspaper photographs of Denis and his scores. That summer of 1947 was when I first played cricket myself at my prep school, but I was much too young to try and copy Compton and Edrich. I just got a liking for it – it came to me and I grabbed hold of it. Also I hit the ball quite well and that probably helped me like it, the fact that I wasn't a complete mug with the bat.

That summer England beat a not very good South African side. I can't imagine there was great interest in the South Africans; they didn't bowl very well, though they did bat well. Alan Melville opened the batting with Bruce Mitchell, both good players who scored hundreds in that series. Dudley Nourse, who averaged over 50 in Test cricket, was playing on that tour as well. He and Melville were named *Wisden* Cricketers of the Year in 1948 for their efforts that summer. Nonetheless, England triumphed 3-0 in the five-Test series.

After a war like we had you were just jolly glad to be alive. In a sense that 1947 summer was a case of rebuilding for the England team. But it wasn't like rebuilding in the modern era, it was a question of trying to get a side to be competitive at the top level after people had died and been wounded.

Len Hutton, Compton and Edrich were all pre-war cricketers but Hedley Verity had gone, Ken Farnes had gone, Hammond had retired. Even Len Hutton had one arm shorter than the other after getting injured during the war and was never quite the same player. Norman Yardley took over from Hammond as captain but had played just one Test prior to the war, while Alec Bedser and Godfrey Evans hadn't played any Test cricket at all.

But although it was a rebuilding process, I don't think it was looked at as that. Everyone was just thoroughly grateful to be there. The relief of being free from the war, that life was returning to normal, is something you can't understate.

It was still a strange time, and the food was filthy. I was lucky enough to live in Norfolk on a farm so the food I had at home was a bit more palatable, but I remember going to boarding school in '47 and the food was almost inedible. But I didn't think of it as inedible because I didn't know much else.

Absolutely everyone watched the County Championship that year. All the grounds were completely full. There weren't anything like the alternatives, there was no television worth speaking about, there were no other attractions and therefore the popularity of cricket was enormous. It's something you can't conceive of now. County Championship matches between Glamorgan and Northamptonshire were pulling in thousands of people a day. Middlesex played Surrey at Lord's in front of 25,000 people.

All the people playing had been in the war, playing for much higher stakes than making runs in the middle, and all of this was reflected. People didn't sledge each other, they played very hard but in a much greater spirit than goes on today.

Middlesex in those days were my side and they won the Championship, beating Gloucestershire narrowly to the title thanks to the efforts of Compton and Edrich. They had a wonderful side and the sun shone throughout. That encapsulates the summer in a nutshell.

It's my golden summer because it was my first in cricket, it was the start of something that blossomed, and because of Edrich and Compton – one my local boy and the other a great hero, the great god of batting.

Henry Blofeld spent 45 years as a commentator on *Test Match Special* before retiring in 2017. He played first-class cricket for Cambridge University.

STEPHEN FAY

1948

BRADMAN'S INVINCIBLES

The former editor of Wisden Cricket Monthly *recalls witnessing arguably Test cricket's greatest side and certainly its most famous dismissal*

This was perhaps the greatest year in the history of cricket. Australian cricket, that is; and their team peaked on a foreign field, or on five fields to be precise – the Test match grounds of post-war England. Australia's captain Don Bradman was the greatest batsman since WG Grace, and for boys growing up in the aftermath of World War II, his team displayed such superiority that a generation became conditioned to living with defeat. The Australians seemed invincible.

It was not just Bradman. Ray Lindwall and Keith Miller were one of the greatest fast-bowling partnerships in the game's history. Miller, who was also a powerful batsman, was an early case of sporting celebrity, who gave schoolboys a glimpse of what glamour might be like. And when one of them was resting, Bill Johnston's left-arm fast-medium spread havoc.

Arthur Morris opened the batting with Syd Barnes, a man of strong opinions to whom rules were a challenge. Lindsay Hassett was shorter and nicer than Bradman; an 18-year-old prodigy named Neil Harvey was also given his chance. I can still feel the awe, just writing those names down.

The only way to watch cricket in 1948 was to go to the match. There was no TV, and ball-by-ball radio commentary was futurology. What we got were intermittent reports from Rex Alston on the BBC, and the late scores which appeared in the Stop Press columns on the back pages of the three London evening papers. Grounds were full, but anyone who turned up early enough simply paid cash at the gate. And sat on the grass.

I was only nine years old, but the second Test in 1948 was at Lord's, and I longed to be there. My father was a journalist in the London office of the *Manchester Guardian*, and he got on well with Denys Rowbotham, the cricket correspondent.

DG Bradman
b WE Hollies 0

Rowbotham met me at the Grace Gate, had a quiet word with someone, and took me to the press box annex, which was square to the wicket in the lower tier of the Grand Stand. It was Saturday, the third day of the second Test.

This was Lord's before its architectural renaissance. The brick building at cow corner where members took tea had an ivy-covered tower. Spectators could stand on raised ground behind the low seats where the Warner Stand now rises. I was speechless when I was introduced to Neville Cardus right there.

The cricket that day was predictably one-sided. Barnes hit sixes into the members' tea-room. Bradman began quietly, but once into his rhythm he scored effortlessly. In my memory, the pair have become the run-stealers, flickering to and fro. Catches were dropped, until Bill Edrich finally held Bradman in the slips on 89. At the close, John Arlott wrote that the game retained no more than an academic interest. Australia went on to win by 409 runs.

I already wanted more, however; and Rowbotham obliged once more at The Oval on my 10th birthday, which was the first day of the fifth Test. On the steps of the press box, he introduced me to Sir Jack Hobbs, a sweet-natured hero who gave me a quick lesson on oiling my bat. It had rained overnight, and when play began at midday Norman Yardley had won the toss and decided to bat. There was, Arlott reported, no evil in the wicket, but Lindwall got the ball to rise steeply, and at lunch, England were 29-4. Only Len Hutton was impervious to the crumbling morale around him. He scored 30 out of 52, England's lowest score against Australia. The great Lindwall had taken 6-20 in 16.1 overs.

That day's cricket is remembered not for England's humiliation, but for Bradman's last Test innings. After a splendid opening partnership of 117, Barnes was out for 61, and Bradman, who needed only four runs to take his Test average beyond 100, was cheered to the wicket. When he was bowled second ball, having misread Eric Hollies' googly, Arlott wondered whether Bradman's eye might not have been a little misted. A momentary shocked silence was followed by another ovation, but feelings were confused. Like most of the crowd, I was delighted to see Bradman out, but simultaneously I felt I had been robbed of a grand climax to his Test career.

As for the tear in his eye, the story of Bradman's last tour suggests that is improbable. Childhood memories undergo alteration, but the thoughtful revisionist history of 1948 written by Malcolm Knox, a distinguished Australian sportswriter and novelist, was published only in 2013. Knox's Bradman is a ruthless, unforgiving leader, determined to take revenge on a team that had scored 903-7 declared against Australia at The Oval only 10 years earlier. He insisted his team should be unbeaten through the whole summer.

Before the tour began, this ambition received a boost by a convenient change in the rule about the availability of the new ball. Previously, the bowling team could take the new ball only after 200 runs had been scored. In November 1947, MCC's rules committee announced that in 1948 the new ball would be available after only 55 overs. The decision was taken after receiving comments from Australia, and Knox reports that two close English friends of Bradman's sat on the rules committee. He drew the inference that they might have been manipulated by an old chum.

The outcome was that the threat from Lindwall and Miller became even more potent. The general feeling that England had been disadvantaged by their fellow countrymen did not go away. In 1998, EW Swanton was still fulminating in *The Cricketer*: "It is hard to believe that England kindly smoothed the path to victory of the 1948 Australians by the availability of the new ball every 55 overs."

History reveals, but it also obscures, and inevitably encourages idle thoughts. Australia won the 1948 series by four Tests, with one drawn. The draw was at Old Trafford, where England led by 141 after the first innings, and left Australia needing to score 317 to win after declaring at 174-3 in the second innings. After three days, Arlott wrote that England were in an impregnable position, probably a winning one. But this was Manchester: it rained throughout the fourth day and most of the fifth. Match drawn.

At Headingley, England's batsmen were on such fine form that Yardley declared their second innings closed again, setting Australia 404 to win in 15 minutes short of six hours. Arlott noted that it was 70 years since a team had won a Test match after their opposition had declared. Unfortunately, England's depleted bowling attack let down the batsmen, and the fielders, by dropping catches, let down the bowlers. Match lost.

Bradman's team was unbeaten in 1948, and the captain became Sir Donald. But when the small boy grew up he could speculate: were Bradman's 'Invincibles' really quite as invincible as history suggests?

Stephen Fay was a former editor of *Wisden Cricket Monthly* and writer for the *Sunday Times*. His book *Arlott, Swanton and the Soul of English Cricket*, co-authored with David Kynaston, was named the *Telegraph*'s Cricket Book of the Year for 2019. Stephen died on May 12, 2020 at the age of 81.

ROD EDMOND

1949

WALTER HADLEE AND HIS KIWI COMPANIONS

New Zealand's performances on their tour of England signalled the end of three-day Test matches and provided comfort in the years of defeats that were to follow

During my childhood in New Zealand in the early 1950s the national cricket team always lost. The nadir was Eden Park, Auckland in 1955 when New Zealand were dismissed for 26, a world-record low to this day. The horror of that collapse stays with me. For a nine-year-old it was almost too much to bear.

My comfort during these torrid years was a book about the 1949 New Zealand tour of England, Alan Mitchell's *Cricket Companions*. I read it over and over, thrilling to the run-scoring feats of the two finest left-handers New Zealand has ever produced, Bert Sutcliffe (2,627 tour runs, average 59.70; 423 runs in the four Tests, average 60.42) and Martin Donnelly (2,287 tour runs; average 61.81, 462 in the Tests, average 77).

In those days a tour was a tour, not a visit. The team of only 15 players came by ship, arrived in April, left in September,

and played 33 first-class matches as well as four Tests. Alan Mitchell travelled with the team, shared their accommodation, and his book conveyed the feel of this exhausting itinerary, the camaraderie especially but also the strain. I was gripped by his account of the captain Walter Hadlee fainting in the dressing room after a hectic run-chase against Derbyshire under a "burning sun".

Re-reading the book all these years later, the consolation and the pride it offered returns as fresh as ever. Every page is familiar. But the tour it describes would be totally unfamiliar to anyone accustomed to seeing half a visiting team fly in from the IPL a couple of days before the first Test. The 1949ers were all amateurs: Hadlee was an accountant, Harry Cave a sheep farmer, CC Burke worked in the Post and Telegraph Department. Their cricket at home was limited to Saturday club matches and three three-day first-class fixtures each season. They enjoyed daily expenses of £1, raised to 30 shillings during the tour.

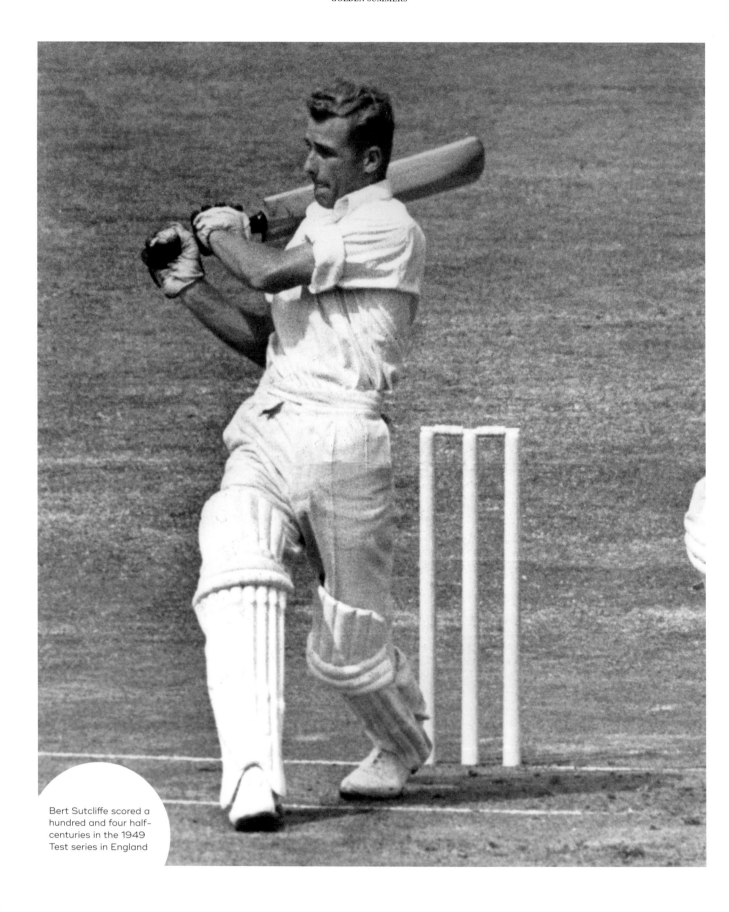

Bert Sutcliffe scored a hundred and four half-centuries in the 1949 Test series in England

Test matches on the tour were limited to three days, something the team resented. It was believed they wouldn't be good enough for anything more, and the counties objected to losing valuable players from Championship matches for any longer than necessary. County cricket had an influence then that has long gone.

The Middlesex players for the first Test at Leeds – Mann the English captain, Compton, Edrich and Young – arrived at 2am on the morning of the first day having come hotfoot from a county match that had finished that evening, a long-ago version of flying in from the IPL.

The three-day Tests resulted in four draws, neither side having the bowling to dismiss strong batting line-ups twice. As draw followed draw England included eight bowlers for the final Test at The Oval but with the same result. Hadlee's team ensured that three-day Tests would never be repeated, although the performance of the next New Zealand team to visit, in 1958, provided grounds for bringing them back.

Mitchell's 'cricket companions' were indeed just that for my childhood self. There was pleasure and relief in reading of a New Zealand team that didn't lose a Test. In fact the only loss on the whole tour, remarkable on the face of it, was to Oxford University. But university cricket was different in those days. Oxford had several internationals, and New Zealand were caught on a sticky wicket. I hated reading the chapter that Mitchell gave to this defeat. But the players were the thing.

I most identified with the youngest member of the team, 20-year-old John Reid, all-rounder *par excellence*. A middle-order batsman, medium-fast seamer and brilliant fielder, it was his ability as reserve wicketkeeper that had clinched his selection for the tour. Reid went on to captain New Zealand's first-ever Test victory, against the West Indies in 1956, and to become probably the country's finest-ever all-rounder. As a student in Wellington in the mid-1960s I used to play at his squash club across the road from the university and inwardly genuflect as he signed me in. But in 1949 he was a work-in-progress and only played in the last two Tests. Mitchell's account of my hero's 93 at The Oval is my favourite passage. Reid died in 2020, the last survivor of a team that so enchanted me.

It was the left-handers, Sutcliffe and Donnelly, however, who most inspired the dogged young left-hander I was becoming.

Sutcliffe's tour aggregate remains second only to Bradman for overseas batsmen in England. He was a natural – lithe, graceful, with exquisite timing in front of the wicket. Cover drives flowed from his bat like a swift-moving river. He was another of the outstanding fielders in the team and a useful left-arm spinner. Years later, when he was 40 and I was 17, I faced him in a club match in Hamilton, too awed to do anything but defend my wicket.

But the player who haunted my imagination, who I was never to see let alone play against, was Martin Donnelly. His innings of 206 at Lord's that summer remains the only double-century by a New Zealander in a Test in England, joining centuries he also made at Lord's for the Dominions against England, Oxford against Cambridge, and Gentlemen versus Players. While at Oxford he also played rugby for England. To cap it all, he was born in Ngaruawahia, just a few miles down the road from my home in Hamilton.

And yet he was hardly seen in New Zealand. Only 13 of his 131 first-class matches were played at home, and none of his seven Tests. He had come to England with the 1937 team as a 19-year-old after only one first-class match. After war service as a tank commander in North Africa and Italy he went on to Oxford from where he joined the 1949 tour.

Having relished Mitchell's account of Donnelly's wonderful summer, the saddest moment of *Cricket Companions* for me was the description of him standing, "a lonely figure on the wharf at Tilbury", when the Rangitata left for home at the end of the tour. This was Donnelly's farewell to New Zealand cricket as well as to his cricket companions. He retired almost immediately and went to live in Australia where he had a successful business career. Donnelly had a twin brother, Maurice, who died as a baby in the Spanish flu epidemic in 1918. Looking back I wonder if there might have been Donnellys to join those other distinguished brothers – Hadlees, Crowes, Bracewells, McCullums – who have graced New Zealand cricket.

And so my golden summer (not a single day was lost through rain) is one that I know only through the bliss of a genre now vanished – the book of the tour.

Rod Edmond is a New Zealand-born academic and Emeritus Professor of Modern Literature and Cultural History at the University of Kent.

DAVID FRITH

1954/55

'TYPHOON' TYSON AND THE BLOW TO THE HEAD THAT CHANGED EVERYTHING

Australia appeared on course for victory in the 1954/55 Ashes, until England's express quick was roused into action

I t's strange but I still see it all in colour. Everything was in its favour: a summer when the memories forged were simply never to fade. I was 17, and my native English loyalty was still strong. Len Hutton and his men had won a famous Ashes victory in 1953, and now here they were in Sydney – admittedly minus Fred Trueman, Jim Laker and Tony Lock, but with two brilliant youngsters in Peter May and Colin Cowdrey, and also Denis Compton on board, and the bowling genius Bob Appleyard, and the left-arm spin magician Johnny Wardle. Also on tour was the lovable, bouncy keeper Godfrey Evans, and the glorious fast-bowling pair of Brian Statham and Frank Tyson, with Alec Bedser unexpectedly and miserably soon to be sidelined after shingles and a bad time in the opening Test at the Gabba.

First sight of the tourists came in the early New South Wales match, during which one remark from a spectator on the old SCG Hill hung awkwardly in the air. His mate asked who this Pommie bloke down on the boundary was. It was Peter Loader. "He's a leg-spinner," murmured that ill-informed gentleman. So much for the supposed wisdom of the Hill regulars.

Billy Watson, a little ginger-haired batsman from my club St George, was called in by New South Wales at the last minute and scored 155 – shedding a quiet tear when he reached three figures. At the end of that summer he won a Test cap. By then, Australia had lost the Ashes (again).

Frank Tyson (right) and Brian Statham lead their team off the field after bowling England to victory at Sydney

England's start to the series could not have been more awful. Len Hutton put Australia in at Brisbane and lost by an innings. This rendered the turnaround in the second Test all the more remarkable.

I don't even need to look at the scorecard. I'm back at the charming old SCG with ease: the old stands ringing the ground, the grassy slope of the Hill crammed with spectators, many eager to display their wit and their knowledge, opposite the most charming pavilion in the world (mercifully still in place today), my heart pounding. Arthur Morris put England in. Hero Hutton was watchful, until deliberately slashing opposing hero Ray Lindwall over the slip cordon. That untypical Hutton stroke was not preserved on film or photograph but resides clearly in my crowded memory bank. Trevor Bailey hung on for some time without scoring before Lindwall's inducker plucked out his middle stump.

But the most dramatic image is of Frank Tyson, batting in a cap, turning away from a Lindwall bouncer, and taking the ball on the back of the head. He went down like a sack of corn and lay still. We thought he was dead. A bunch of British sailors to my left yelled out indignantly. It was an intensely worrying time. Some minutes later Tyson slowly regained his feet and was helped off by the St John Ambulance chaps. Nobody could have foreseen then that 'Typhoon' Tyson would blast his way to 10 wickets in this delectable match.

Tellingly, Wardle at No.9 top-scored with a slashing 35, dragging England up to 154 with a last-wicket stand of 43 with Statham, the highest of the innings. Australia (228) then took an ominous 74-run lead and reduced England to 55-3 second time round, before the university boys May (104 in five hours) and Cowdrey (54) rescued the innings. That left Australia seeking 223 to go two up in the series – but only after Statham and this time Appleyard had raised a fateful 46 for England's 10th wicket.

On the fifth day, Tyson made the headlines: 6-85 to go with his 4-45. There had been visual evidence that some of the Australians were genuinely scared of him. That knock on the head seemed to have changed everything. England by 38 runs, series one-all with three to play.

The Englishmen were back in town seven weeks later, having retained the Ashes with victories at Melbourne (Cowdrey 102, Tyson 7-27) and Adelaide. With television still a few years in the future, it was the radio which sustained us all, together with the newsreel cinemas. I wasn't able to see any of the second New South Wales match in mid-February, which was a pity because it was drama-packed too: NSW, led by Keith Miller, five down for 26 on the opening day yet going on to beat Hutton's men by 45 runs, match top-score going to 19-year-old Bob Simpson (98). On the Sunday rest day the England team were said to be coming down to Cronulla for a barbecue laid on by the golf club. They didn't show up, and momentarily I was bitter. But soon the final Test was scheduled to start. And on three days I took the train into Sydney, walked across

Moore Park, and waited with everyone else until play was called off. When it rains in Sydney it really does rain.

That left three days, and what fun they produced. It was the last time I was to see my batting hero, Len Hutton, at the crease. Having made 6 he glanced Lindwall to a tense debutant Peter Burge for a well-executed dismissal. The other opener was none other than Tom Graveney, and he and May put on 182. Tom made his only Ashes century. The decisive over remains vivid in the memory: drinks, and a very flushed Graveney, 86 not out, removed his cap and wiped himself with a towel. Upon resumption Miller's eight-ball over went for four fours as Graveney drove and swept his way to his hundred. An elderly man alongside me on the splintery benches at the Paddington End kept remarking on Graveney's resemblance to a previous Gloucestershire and England batsman, Charlie Barnett.

There was a bonus: Compton got going at last, having tossed his cap to the square-leg umpire. The sweep and the drive got him to 84. Bailey made 72 before gifting his wicket to Lindwall, who, with 99 wickets, was not expected to play against England again. (He was still around four years later, and inflicted a 'pair' on Bailey at Melbourne.)

Australia just failed to avoid the follow-on, Ian Johnson and Lindwall getting into a hilarious mix-up with one run needed to avoid it, and Hutton sent them in again with just under two hours of the match left (no minimum number of overs in those days). England still got through nearly 30 eight-ball overs in that time, and there was some fun and games along the way. Graveney took his only Test wicket (the stubborn Colin McDonald). Tyson, coming in off a run-up of only a few paces, knocked Miller's bat from his hands. And Wardle continued to muddle the Aussies with his left-arm wrist-spin, to a chorus of "Coom on ye broad acres!" from the English sailors.

Nothing was more emotional than the final over. Captain Hutton himself walked slowly across the field of play, removed his cap, set his field, and bowled to Richie Benaud. They were not all that well disposed to each other. The English veteran had teased him often as he struggled through his early Ashes Tests. Benaud now decided to have the last word. He would plant the Yorkshireman's rolled leg-break onto the pavilion clock. He heaved. He missed. Benaud b Hutton 22. Series ended. Australia 1, England 3.

I wasn't going to run off home. I hung around, catching sight of Tyson and Graveney draped in towels in the visitors' dressing room, standing close to John Arlott (with whom I would one day have a deep friendship) as he irritably told a boy that he was not Denis Compton, and later positioning myself exactly 22 yards away as Frank 'Typhoon' Tyson strolled down the pathway to the rear of the pavilion.

I was inconsolable, for the tour was over and my heroes would soon be flying away. I would not have felt so flat had I known that sometime in the future I'd be well acquainted with almost every one of the players – on both sides.

And, to this day, visions from that 1954/55 golden summer can be called up in my mind's eye at any time: and all in full colour.

David Frith is the author of over 30 cricket books and former editor of *The Cricketer* and *Wisden Cricket Monthly*. His loyalties continue to swing back and forth between England and Australia.

TED DEXTER

1960

COMING OUT SWINGING

After the austere Fifties, a new decade called for a different kind of style;
English cricket had just the man

T he year began with great success in the West Indies, on a tour where I scored more runs for England than anyone else. I'd already made my maiden Test hundred the winter before against New Zealand, but the runs I made in the Caribbean felt more significant, just for the quality of the opposition.

It was all so new and exciting, playing at these great venues. We were the MCC team in those days and we were expected to sell the game to the locals. The crowds were so vocal, especially at Barbados, where I made my first hundred. It was a rather flat pitch, but nevertheless they had three good quick bowlers – I batted at No.6 and the score wasn't looking too healthy when I went out in our first innings, but Wes Hall soon took the new ball and that whistled to the boundary. It was the first of many

invigorating battles I would have with Wes. In reply Garry Sobers and Frank Worrell batted for seven sessions!

I made another hundred in the series, at Guyana on a slow turner. I batted most of the time with Raman Subba Row, a wise old head who helped me through that innings. I made my mark on that tour, and arrived back in England to take over the captaincy of Sussex from Robin Marlar.

I was ready for it. I'd captained my school Radley and then Cambridge University, I'd been well trained and I brought that to bear. There was no great method, I just encouraged people to show their best. I used to say, "Just go out and show them how bloody good you are!".

Early in 1960 I made a lot of runs along with Jim Parks. Both of us were in the running to make 1,000 runs by the end of May. By May 11th I'd made 429; by the 18th I'd made 721. At that time I thought I was pretty much nailed-on, but then there was

Dexter, stepping out as captain of Cambridge University

some weather interruptions and neither of us quite made it, but it was pretty exciting.

As captain we won five of my first seven Championship matches. We beat Surrey for the first time since 1947. The records tell me that Dexter made 135 and Parks 155, in a match we won by an innings. Surrey had been the team to beat in the Fifties – they and Yorkshire had been scrapping it out since forever. Sussex on the other hand were a lowly lot, so it was a significant victory. It showed we could play with those grand institutions of the game.

We ended up finishing fourth in the County Championship, winning 12 of our 32 matches. I played in 20 games and made 1,771 runs at an average of 55 and took 33 wickets. Sussex put on 1,200 new members and gate receipts went up by £2,000, which is the equivalent of £45,000 now. It was a truly golden summer.

Our great fast bowler John Snow hadn't even appeared yet; he would debut the following year. With Snowy, or even just another spinner, we could have won the Championship. In those days on uncovered pitches you really needed a couple of spinners to win games. I had Ian Thomson, who made one tour for England, a super bowler who got his wickets every year, and Don Bates and Tony Buss, all good seamers. I had one slow-left arm spinner in Ronnie Bell, who I looked after. He was a lovely spinner who I loved to let bowl, but he wasn't the greatest. We did superbly well with pretty modest resources.

I played for England that summer too. South Africa were in town, and we had a marvellously talented team. Cowdrey, Barrington, Parks, Subba Row, a young Ray Illingworth, Trueman, Statham. That was some side, and the cricket we played was very serious. Peter May was my captain for much of my early Test career and he handled me very well. I was a bit flighty, a bit chancy, and he used to play along with that. He didn't try to knock me into shape. He'd just say, "Come on Edward, let's see what you've got up your sleeve today!".

I didn't make many runs, we won the games pretty easily because their batting was poor but there was nothing wrong with their attack. They were low-scoring matches. Neil Adcock and Hughie Tayfield were fantastic bowlers. And of course there was Geoff Griffin, the chucker. He bowled me out at Lord's, I hadn't played against him before and the ball just appeared out of nowhere. Lord's back then, batting at the Nursery End, was a nightmare. I don't know how anybody got any runs. There were no sightscreens, just a red-brick pavilion with spectators in coloured blazers. These days if someone picks their nose by the side of the sightscreen the whole game is stopped!

It was around that time that I got to know Freddie Trueman. I'd barely met the man before being called out late for the Ashes tour of 1958/59. In those days we all had to share rooms but there was an odd one out, and they had decided to let Fred have a room to himself so he could get up to whatever tricks he

fancied. And then I suddenly appear, and they couldn't give us two single rooms so I was put in with Freddie. That was quite a culture shock…

We got on fine, Fred and I. The only slight problem we had, and it was something that scribes tended to pick up on, came later in the decade, when he lost half his bonus on the 1962/63 Ashes tour. As captain I thought that was what he deserved, after he didn't turn up on the most important morning of the Melbourne Test match. It was half an hour before play was due to start, and he was nowhere. I looked around, "Where's Freddie?" I asked if anyone had seen him at breakfast, but no one had. The game was there to be won and he was our No.1 player! God knows what he'd been up to, but what I do know is he'd taken two wickets overnight, and the ball was still quite new. So I was thinking of giving him the ball first thing in the morning.

Finally, with minutes to spare, he shows up. It was eight-ball overs back then, so he runs in to bowl and halfway through the over I'm looking at him and he's puffing away. By the sixth ball, it was hardly reaching the wicketkeeper, he was absolutely bust. "OK, Fred, thanks very much." I'd already decided to give him the second new ball when it came around, so I moved him around in the field and kept him in the shade until we were able to take that new ball. He took it and got the job done, and we end up winning the game. I can still remember Swanton's article in the *Telegraph*: "Only the young and inexperienced England captain can possibly explain how he failed to bowl Trueman, our best bowler, for most of the day…"

It was just a special time. I was young, I was enjoying what I was doing, and my dad was paying the bills! I'd gotten married to Susan in 1959 – though the honeymoon was cut short to play for Sussex against Worcester. We weren't that well off; Susan was earning good money modelling, and that was an important part of our income. She probably didn't enjoy it so much when I had £5 each way on a loser! It was quite a lively time, London was starting to perk up a bit, although the effects of the war lingered for a hell of a long time. After all, rationing was still there in the mid-Fifties.

We lived in Pimlico in a little flat that my dad bought us, and I could walk to Victoria, catch the 9am Bright Belle and be at the ground at Hove at 10.15am. I'd sit in my first-class seat in the corner and my *Telegraph* would be waiting for me: "Good morning, Mr Dexter, your usual, sir?" Life felt pretty good. It was better than being in the army, that was for sure. The Sixties were just getting going, and things were rolling our way.

Ted Dexter is a former England captain, chairman of selectors, pilot, writer, businessman, would-be politician and plenty more besides. His autobiography, 85 Not Out, is out now, with all proceeds going to the MCC Foundation.

STEPHEN
BRENKLEY

1964

BEING KENNY

*The snail-paced Ashes series of 1964 was forgettable to most who saw it,
but the immovable Ken Barrington proved an inspiration*

y common consent the fourth Test of the 1964 Ashes series was a turgid disgrace. Not in our house, it wasn't. We watched the match when we could, we listened to it, we thought about it. During it and for weeks afterwards we played it again and then replayed it.

It was the week, the long week, when Ken Barrington confirmed the place he still occupies in my consciousness along with a few others such as Derek Underwood, Tony Greig, Alan Knott and modern heroes who will go unmentioned to spare all our blushes. Not a week goes by – in truth, it may be more like a day – when Kenny and his chums from Old Trafford do not surface in the mind's eye.

The match, which you may have tried to forget if you were around, and never to dwell on for more than an incredulous glance at the scorebook if you were not, began on a hot Thursday in July. The sun shone almost throughout and by the following

Tuesday, a draw, the only probable result from around lunch on the first day, was officially declared.

Australia, winning the toss for the only time in the series, made 656-8 declared from 255.5 overs and England replied with 611 all out from 293.1, which left time only for two overs of the tourists' second innings. Bobby Simpson made 311 for Australia, his first Test hundred at the 52nd attempt, still the longest wait for a specialist Australian batsman, and Barrington scored 256 for England, his first Test century at home – following nine abroad – at the 45th time of asking, a delay surpassed only by Mark Ramprakash's 54 innings.

The sun also shone for the duration on the green at Reeth, the small village in Swaledale in the North Riding of Yorkshire where we lived. The green was split, as it still is, into three sections. Unlike now, when cars are parked on the turf for much of the summer and small boys no longer automatically gravitate there with bat and ball and would be frowned on for doing so, we – my two brothers and three or four pals – played cricket there every day and night on two pitches which we had constructed by default.

Our preferred venue was across the cobbles directly opposite the Kings Arms Hotel, which our parents owned and ran. They were perpetually busy in those high-summer days, looking after the needs of residents at breakfast, providing high teas for the holidaymakers who were passing through and then looking after a busy bar and dining room in the evening. My brothers and I were left to our own devices and were glad of it.

Sport dominated our young lives in Reeth but there was no question of playing anything other than cricket in high summer. My first concrete memory of big-time cricket is from 1961 when my mum, who loved it, lamented one afternoon in August: "May's out for a duck, we're in trouble now all right." Not quite sure what she meant then, I now know it was the England captain Peter May being bowled by Richie Benaud second ball at the start of England's collapse against Australia at Old Trafford. She was absolutely correct, we *were* in trouble all right.

Two years later, at Reeth's annual summer show, I entered the children's fancy dress competition, dressed in flannels and swathed in bandages, as One of the Ruins that Charlie Griffith Knocked About a Bit, in homage to the damage inflicted on England's batsmen that 1963 summer by the West Indies fast bowler. It still rankles slightly that the outfit went unrewarded.

By the following summer, which brought the arrival of the Aussies, cricket had started to become the first thing I thought of on waking up in the morning and the last thing on pulling over the bed covers at night. Over the years since, that has not changed much.

The point for us was not really what was happening in Manchester, though we understood well enough that if Australia engineered a draw they would retain the Ashes because they had won the third Test in Leeds. Our focus was on re-enacting the deeds of the players on our prized strip of turf. We had an old bat, which belonged to the village, a mixture of tennis and cork balls, and beer crates from my dad's cellar for stumps.

Although I rather fancied myself as a bowler in those days – and indeed still spend the winters' dreams working on a mystery ball that will bamboozle all batsmen and lead to Test selection overnight – it was Barrington I was soon eager to emulate. After Australia had posted their huge total, England were in the relatively parlous position of 126-2. Enter Barrington an hour before the close on the third day. We watched him until the end of play and then went out to the green to be him. Or that was the idea. I batted first, my elder brother bowled, the younger was behind the wicket. It might sound jolly decent of Al to have let his middle sibling go in first, but he knew how it would turn out. I lasted for about six balls before the beer crate went tumbling over. His turn to bat.

He was still there when we were called in around 9pm. The following morning, we watched the Test for an hour and then went to the green. Al resumed his innings and eventually declared because he was thirsty. Kenny was showing no such inclination.

At the close of the fourth day, Barrington was 173 not out, having lost Ted Dexter for 174 not long before, ending a partnership of 246. By then he was a god in my eyes, a status that has never really diminished. The Ashes were lost but that hardly mattered to an 11-year-old boy who was watching and feeling an Englishman bat and bat as though his life depended on it. The criticism being offered by the newspapers was of no significance.

That summer and that match were a huge part of the rite of cricketing passage. We found we rather admired Worcestershire's challenge in the Championship despite living where we did. Even then, it seemed something for a county to be winning the title for the first time. And they had Tom Graveney, another hero. Graveney scored more runs than any other batsman that summer, including his 100th hundred. We were not alone in wondering why he was not playing for England.

It was Jim Standen, however, who exercised our attention as much as anyone. In May of that year Standen was West Ham's goalkeeper when they won a celebrated FA Cup final against Preston. Three weeks later he was in Worcestershire's side as their (usually) first-change seam bowler. He was the leader of the Championship averages. For this all-round prowess, Standen harboured almost a similar place in my heart to Barrington.

At Cape Town in 2016 when Ben Stokes was plundering the South African bowlers and scoring the fastest 250 in all Tests, I thought longingly of Kenny, whose 250 remains the second slowest. It was an unfettered privilege to see Stokes; it was part of life's passage to watch and, for a little while on Reeth Green, to be Barrington.

Stephen Brenkley is a former cricket correspondent for the *Independent*, the *Independent on Sunday* and the *Evening Standard*.

Ken Barrington averaged 58.67 in Test cricket, scoring 20 hundreds

STEPHEN
CHALKE

1966

SOBERS TAKES
CENTRE STAGE

*The summer of 1966 witnessed the game's greatest all-rounder
at the very peak of his powers*

The West Indians were not supposed to tour again till 1971. But their visit in 1963 had been such a triumph that South Africa got pushed into sharing a summer with New Zealand, and back came the West Indians, only three years on from their last tour.

I was 15 years old in 1963, and the Lord's Test that year caught my imagination as no other Test has ever done. There was a magnificence about the tall, muscular Wes Hall, coming in over after over on his long run, bowling into the evening till his last drop of energy was almost spent. There was a thrilling madness about the way the balding Brian Close came down the wicket to him and, thrashing away, almost won the game. And the drama of the last over, when Colin Cowdrey came out with his arm in plaster, it was like a 'Roy of the Rovers' story from the *Tiger* comic.

Three years on, in the summer of 1966, I was between school and university, living out my confused Christianity by working in a hospital for the 'severely subnormal' near St Albans. I was away from home and lonely, with a room in the nurses' quarters, and I looked forward to my Saturdays when I went down to London – to the theatre or to Lord's.

I wanted to see my favourite players. When it was Sussex, that meant Ted Dexter, Jim Parks and the Nawab of Pataudi, all attractive strokemakers. Sussex had won the toss and were batting – hooray! I settled down in the Grand Stand, and I watched in dismay as, within the space of an over, a medium-pace bowler called Hooker dismissed all three of them for ducks. I ended up at the Haymarket Theatre, watching Shaw's *You Never Can Tell*. I retain no picture of Hooker, but I can still hear Ralph Richardson's amused voice: "You never can tell, sir. You never can tell."

Brian Close and
Garfield Sobers toss
up at The Oval ahead
of the fifth Test

Dexter played only three games that summer. Peter May had long retired, and Fred Trueman was past his best. English cricket was crying out for a new generation of entertainers, and it found one in the rotund figure of Colin Milburn, a swashbuckling batsman with an infectious grin. He was picked for the first Test at Old Trafford and, after being run out for nought in the first innings, hit a joyous 94 that eased the pain of losing in three days. The only other batsman to make runs was Cowdrey, another who would not pass today's bleep test. That was part of the charm of English cricket in those days; the players came in all shapes and sizes.

The West Indians were different. Unlike most English cricketers they seemed to play without inhibition, none more so than Garry Sobers. As summer went on, and he piled glory upon glory, he became my hero. Alas, I arrived too late to get into the Saturday of the Lord's Test, when Tom Graveney – recalled once more – hit 96. So I persuaded my father to buy us a pair of advance tickets for The Oval.

I worked from Monday to Friday in Ward Six, a heavily locked villa which housed 40 children, most of whom were unable to speak, some bedridden. A bright, little lad called David had been given a cricket set by his parents, and I tried to set up games with him on the high-fenced back lawn. But it was not a great success; I was forever coaxing the rubber ball out of the mouths of other children.

It was a relief when the day was over; I could get back to my room and tune my transistor radio to the last hour of the Test. On the Monday at Lord's, West Indies were five wickets down in their second innings and only nine runs ahead. Then Sobers and his cousin David Holford put on 274.

I had a week off in early August for my brother's wedding. I was the best man, and all day I wanted to know the score from Headingley. We were losing again, after another Sobers century, but Basil D'Oliveira was batting well. He was another of my heroes that summer, his life-story a triumph over the hateful apartheid. It was uplifting the way everybody in England warmed to him.

At The Oval I sat with Dad in the East Stand, and it was not at all the day I had anticipated. Tom Graveney and John Murray scored hundreds. Wes Hall and Charlie Griffith, so potent all summer, looked weary, and England's last pair, John Snow and Ken Higgs, amid great cheers, broke all sorts of records with a stand of 128. So great had been the West Indian dominance all summer that Higgs was the only man left from the team for the first Test. By close West Indies had lost four second-innings wickets, and they were still 124 behind.

Sobers had yet to bat, and I was desperate to see him. His average for the series was 120, and I was certain that once more he would save the game with a glorious century. And I so much wanted to be there when he did it. I went back to the hospital, worked on Sunday and returned to The Oval, together with a friend from school. Just before the 11.30 start we sat down on the terrace in front of the gasometers.

By 11.50 West Indies had lost three wickets, including Sobers first ball, hooking Snow and caught at short-leg by England's new captain, the brilliantly mad Brian Close. West Indian supporters were still arriving, full of excitement; they all went quiet when they saw the scoreboard. Sobers, nought? It was not possible.

The game was over soon after lunch. We joined the crowd in front of the pavilion, then took the tube to Oxford Street, where we watched Olivier's *Hamlet* in the Academy Cinema. It's a very good film, but I would rather have seen Sobers score a century.

He is the supreme cricketer of my lifetime, and that was his greatest summer.

Stephen Chalke's first book, *Runs in the Memory*, was Frank Keating's Sports Book of the Year in the *Guardian* in 1998. Four of his titles have won Cricket Book of the Year awards: two from *Wisden*, one from the Cricket Society and one from the National Sporting Club. He founded Fairfield Books and in 2019 received the Peter Smith Award from the Cricket Writers' Club for outstanding presentation of cricket to the public.

CHRISTOPHER SANDFORD

1967

THE VELVET GLOVES OF JT MURRAY

The glovework of a natural wicketkeeper struggled to convince England's selectors he was worthy of his place

The year 1967 was my own private summer of love, but not for any reasons connected with the world of herbally-tinged joss sticks or bare-thighed young women swaggering around London's Carnaby Street in their Mary Quant miniskirts. Social ferment was slow to disturb St Aubyns prep school in Rottingdean, East Sussex, where as a 10-year-old I found myself detained for much of that supposedly swinging era.

The school itself was a combination of distressed seaside hotel and Victorian fortress, with innumerable outbuildings and corridors, all smelling obscurely of boiled cabbage, grouped around the central block, and a sturdy flint wall separating the whole place from a large, randomly mown playing field, that, like Lord's, rolled drunkenly down from north to south. That was

probably its only point of resemblance to cricket's headquarters.

Brambles abounded in the St Aubyns outfield, which was rumoured to have been further disfigured by a Luftwaffe bomb, and a stiff sea breeze sometimes knocked over deckchairs and sent empty crisp packets eddying around as if the old Brighton Belle had just passed by the platform.

As I say, though, there was love in the air during that summer of 1967, and in my case this meant cricket in general and more particularly the incumbent England wicketkeeper John 'JT' Murray. Murray was exquisite. The sheer class of the man communicated itself even on the boxy, black-and-white Baird TV set perched in a distant corner of the St Aubyns schoolroom where I principally watched him.

He seemed to me to be much like Cary Grant with gauntlets. Always immaculately turned out in creamy white flannels and

John 'JT' Murray played 21 Tests for England between 1961 and 1967

a blue cap, Murray would go through a little routine before each ball was bowled, circling his arms, the tips of the gloves touched together, patting the peak of the cap, and then dropping smoothly down to settle on his haunches behind the stumps. There was something both athletic and sedate about his posture. Some people, the England selectors apparently among them, seemed to have their doubts about Murray's batting, but this was not a particular issue to those of us who had seen him take a scorching 112 off the fearsome West Indies attack in the previous year's final Test at The Oval.

India, under their dashing, one-eyed captain the Nawab of Pataudi, were the first of the two tourists to face England that summer.

Rain played havoc with the visitors' warm-up matches, although Pataudi himself scored an unbeaten 144 against his old colleagues at Oxford University and an even-time 70 (more than half his side's total) against a strong MCC attack at Lord's.

Geoff Boycott remained unbeaten on 246, scored in 573 minutes, when England closed their innings at 550-4 in the first Test at Headingley. The Indians were beaten by six wickets, but Boycott was then promptly dropped from the side for "selfish batting". The go-ahead chairman of selectors, Doug Insole, and his panel evidently felt that the Yorkshireman's marathon knock failed to advance the cause of the "brighter cricket" they had promised the public. In other circumstances, he might have been hailed as a national hero.

England won the next Test at Lord's, too: my man Murray picked up six catches in the visitors' first innings, which equalled the wicketkeeping world record. He later genially told me that he was "reasonably sure" (he may have added a choice intensifier or two) that three of his rejected appeals were also out, which, if true, would have made for an impressive haul of nine dismissals. Tom Graveney, having just that week turned 40, celebrated his own personal Indian summer by scoring a chanceless 151 in the first and only England innings.

Murray then proceeded to add the Batsman of the Match award in the third Test at Edgbaston, where he top-scored with 77 out of an England total of 298. India were shot out for 92, and went on to lose by 132 runs. It was all highly satisfactory if, like me, you fanatically supported the home team in general and their suave wicketkeeper-batsman in particular.

The side seemed to have it all – batsmen as variously talented as Barrington, Milburn and Graveney, an opening attack of Snow and Brown, and in Brian Close one of the greatest and most astute of captains in marshalling that strength to its most effective use.

Regrettably, things rather went downhill from there. Just 10 days after impressing with the bat at Edgbaston, Murray suffered the ignominy of scoring a pair in the first Test against Pakistan at Lord's. In fairness it might be added that the ball generally dominated the bat in that game, where it rained heavily on each of the five days (despite which, Pakistan's captain Hanif Mohammad accumulated a nine-hour, unbeaten 187), and also that *The Times* expressed a widely held view when it reported that the England wicketkeeping had been "very high class" and "superbly neat" throughout. The match itself was drawn.

Nonetheless, there was a shock coming when on August 6 the team was announced for the second Test at Trent Bridge. Murray was out. So were five other members of the side that had acquitted itself well at Lord's. No fewer than eight of the England players who had started the Test series in early June would be gone by the time it finished in late August. To call Insole – a fine amateur cricketer in his day, and an undeniably conscientious official – the David Bowie of the sports administration world would perhaps be to confer a flattering sense of consistency on a man who seemed to restlessly chop and change his team with each successive match in search of an elusive balance between the aesthetically pleasing and the statistically successful.

Anyway, England went on to win both at Trent Bridge and in the summer's final Test at The Oval. The wonderfully gritty, flat-nosed Ken Barrington scored a lot of runs, and bowlers like Derek Underwood and Geoff Arnold, the latter making his Test debut, skilfully exploited the damp conditions. It has to be said that Murray's replacement, the young Kent stumper Alan Knott, proved more than competent at least when standing back to the seamers. It's a moot point whether he ever touched the classical heights routinely achieved by my hero, but set against this he was also thought to be more nudgingly creative with the bat.

In all, then, perhaps more of a bittersweet summer than a strictly golden one, but I did have the end-of-holiday consolation of seeing Mike Denness score a brisk half-century for Kent and 48-year-old Bill Alley take 3-22 for Somerset in the Gillette Cup final at a drizzly but noisily partisan Lord's.

Meanwhile, Yorkshire won their second consecutive Championship title, although Insole and his co-selectors then decided to axe Brian Close (with a Test captaincy record of six wins and a draw) after he supposedly wasted time in a county match at Edgbaston his side might otherwise have lost. The nation was polarised between those who thought Close had it coming, and others (the player himself among them) who felt it had more to do with the effete, southern cricketing establishment ridding itself of a horny-handed, northern professional. In either case, an MCC party, without either Close or Murray in its ranks, set off under Colin Cowdrey's captaincy for what proved to be a thrilling winter tour of the West Indies. But that's another story.

Christopher Sandford has published biographies of Imran Khan, Mick Jagger and John F Kennedy, among others, and has worked as a film and music writer and reviewer for more than 20 years.

SURESH MENON

1967/68

INDIA'S AWAKENING

India's 1967/68 Test series in Australia was a formative one for both the national team and our author

"**A**nd then Bradman's pitiless blade went into action again." That's a very confusing sentence for a young boy to read. I hadn't actually watched a proper cricket match yet – not at first-class level, not at club level, nothing. The only cricket I had played was with my sister in the veranda of our house. The rules were simple. There were 'stumps' (doors) at either end. If the bowler hit the batsman's stumps, he (or she) was out; if the batsman hit the bowler's stumps, then the bowler was out and now had to bat.

But two things happened that summer of 1967.

I discovered proper cricket. First in the pages of a sports magazine, and then on radio where I followed my first Test series. The magazine *Sport & Pastime* was serialising Ralph Barker's two books, *Ten Great Innings* and *Ten Great Bowlers*. My early heroes thus were Spofforth and Grace and Ranji and MacLaren and Spooner and Lohmann. Summer is relative. It wasn't

actually summer in Bangalore where I lived, but such is the sun's generosity that it is bound to be summer somewhere. In that year of awakening, the summer was in Australia, as India played a Test in Adelaide over Christmas.

False memories are a fan's best friend. Bradman's pitiless blade might have had nothing to do with Ralph Barker. More likely, it had to do with Jack Fingleton, who wrote for the magazine. I spent days wondering if it referred to Bradman the batsman or Bradman the incessant shaver.

"This thing," said Spofforth, "can be done." I marvelled at the certainty of an Australian bowler who could personally ensure that England would not score the 85 runs needed for a win. In my early years, I had total recall. I could remember whole pages that I read. Today it isn't the words that I remember so much as the emotions: my madeleine, unlocking memory in the Proustian manner.

I remember my mother, ear fixed to the radio, keeping scores as Farokh Engineer and Chandu Borde put on a partnership. Every time she rushed into the kitchen and rushed back again, Engineer

Bishan Bedi, India's majestic left-arm spinner, pictured at New Road, Worcester in 1967

had hit a boundary. Mother was the only lady I knew who kept scores and updated friends who were at work. She taught me the joy of listening to cricket. The sport was an audio treat before it became a visual one. When Dad came back from work, they would discuss the day's play. Dad and Mom fired a boy's imagination, helped by an uncle who knew his cricket, having actually played the game.

Family heroes began to emerge. Erapalli Prasanna, who claimed 25 wickets in that series and brought India back into the match at Adelaide numerous times. ML Jaisimha, who arrived in Brisbane one afternoon and scored a Test match century the next day. Engineer, Ajit Wadekar, Bishan Bedi, and, above all, the captain, Nawab of Pataudi, who missed the first Test and finished with scores of 75 and 85, 74 and 48, 51 and 6 – I haven't had to look these up! That 74 was in Brisbane where he shared the top score with Jaisimha; the 48 was a let-down. A few more, and India might have won the Test they lost by just 39 runs. Fingleton wrote that India could have won two Tests.

Pataudi was to say later that the Australians were not as good as the 4-0 scoreline suggested, and that if the series had begun with the Brisbane Test, the result might have been different. He was probably right, since India followed that with a 3-1 victory in New Zealand, their first series victory abroad (the West Indies under Garry Sobers who toured next could only draw the series 1-1).

But that 1967 tour of Australia was important, and not just for firing the imagination of a seven-year-old thousands of kilometres away. It was – despite the defeat – the first step India took to coming together as a team and demanding a place at the high table, something that would be conceded with series wins in the West Indies and England three years later.

A world-class spin combination came together. Spearhead of the attack, leg-spinner Bhagwat Chandrasekhar, had to return to India after breaking down in the first Test. That brought the focus to bear upon off-spinner Prasanna, who finished with 49 wickets in the twin series. India's strengths and weaknesses were both on public display – the reliance on spin, and the woeful catching. Bob Cowper and Ian Chappell made big centuries aided by dropped catches.

On one horrendous occasion, two fielders running for a catch – Rusi Surti and V Subramanya – clashed, and the latter broke his nose.

That was another memory of that period. For when Subramanya returned to Bangalore, he underwent treatment at the same orthopaedic hospital where an aunt of mine was having surgery.

"Do you want to meet a Test cricketer?" my father asked. He had checked with Subramanya, who had kindly agreed. I can remember the feel of Dad's hand as I slipped mine into it. Subramanya, nose bandaged and thus speaking strangely, greeted me warmly. His was the first Test star's hand I shook, a story I lived off for a while. Decades later at a cricket function in Bangalore, I narrated this story to Subbu (familiarity breeds contraction), and his spontaneous response was, "Of course I remember that handshake". Lovely man.

Ian Peebles has written about the impact of cricket as seen through 12-year-old eyes. That's nothing compared to the impact of the game on seven-year-old ears. Was Lindsay Hassett one of the commentators? I don't remember. There was an Indian on that panel, V Chakrapani, whom I met briefly many years later in Chennai, a tall man who moved easily and spoke in a beautiful radio voice.

Over the years, members of the squad became good friends. Tiger Pataudi himself, more laid-back than David Gower and a conversation-stopper whenever he entered a room. Bedi, whose biography I wrote a few years ago. The late Jaisimha, in whose company I watched junior matches and who occasionally came down from a commentary box to compare impressions. Prasanna, who told me when I first began reporting, "I shall be keeping an eye on you". Wadekar, whose room on international tours when he was manager was "liberty hall", open to friend and foe alike.

Summer of '67 was also when I decided that I would play for India one day. I calculated that some of the players on that Australian tour would be my colleagues when I made my debut 10 years later (in my mind I was a child prodigy). Sadly, I went from being a promising youngster to a has-been without a significant career in between. These things happen.

But such disappointment was in the future; meanwhile, there was Bradman's pitiless blade and Spofforth's promise to focus on. And before the season was done, I had discovered new heroes closer to home, living and breathing ones at that.

Suresh Menon is an Indian journalist, author and sportswriter. He was formerly editor of the *Wisden India Almanack*.

PAUL EDWARDS

1975

WIND OF CHANGE

Clive Lloyd bestrode the summer of 1975 like a colossus, as his West Indies side won the inaugural men's World Cup

Saturday, May 31, 1975. Buxton. Clive Lloyd. This graceful giant of a man is demolishing Derbyshire's bowling. His bat weighs three pounds and plenty, yet every ounce obeys him. Balls are not so much lost as permanently exiled. Lloyd is not simply taller than everyone else; he seems to become freakishly bigger on this club ground, almost a cartoon figure bestriding his miniature world. He finishes with 167 not out in Lancashire's 477-5, innings closed after 100 overs. In the tea interval I bought Andy Mayne, my former English teacher, a half of bitter in the beer tent. He deserved much more. It snowed on the Monday, the first Monday in June.

Letters and reading lists had arrived that January, telling me I needed my own copies of works by the Venerable Bede and Alexis de Tocqueville, but I would ignore this worthy advice, for I already knew the books I wanted to buy; their authors included

FS Ashley-Cooper, John Arlott and Alan Ross. University could wait; it was the cricket season.

It was a summer of confinement and freedom. The restriction came early when Dad decided that I should do some proper work and got me a job at the Department of Employment in Manchester's Aytoun Street. For two spirit-numbing months I filled in forms with lists of figures and tried to make completed innings out of every group of 11. I left in something like mid-June, resolved that whatever I did with my life would have a trifle more purpose to it. Cricket writing, though? Never gave it a thought.

Which was odd, because I was already lost to the game. I had mourned the death of Neville Cardus in February and spent most of my dosh on cricket books from Gibb's or Shaw's or from a stall up Shudehill. In the days when even wartime *Wisdens* cost only a few quid I regularly arrived home with bags of treasure. "Where's all this cricket going to get you?" asked Mum.

It was something of a Janus summer. The first World Cup portended increased international competition, particularly in limited-overs games, although the changes triggered by the Packer revolution lay nearly two years ahead. Exactly three weeks after pummelling Fred Swarbrook and his mates at Buxton, Lloyd was making another century, watched this time by 26,000 spectators in the World Cup final at Lord's. The West Indies skipper helped his team score 291-8 in 60 overs, a monstrous score in those days and 17 runs too many for Ian Chappell's Australia, who had beaten England in the semi-final at Headingley.

In that game Gary Gilmour first took 6-14 as the hosts were bowled out for 93 on the greenest of pitches, before whacking 28 not out to rescue his team from 39-6. And, as I revisit that old scorecard, suddenly there's Chris Old pointing gleefully at the single bail he's just dislodged to dismiss Rod Marsh. Dad and I are watching our TV in the lounge and wondering if the match can be won after all.

Yet for all the ruckus of the new, the gentle rhythms of the '75 English season would still have been recognisable to someone who had stopped watching the game a decade earlier. There was a four-match Ashes series to savour, although 'gentle' is scarcely the word to describe Tests which featured Dennis Lillee and Jeff Thomson in their savage pomp. To combat this threat, England had called up David Steele, 33, bespectacled, a county pro from Northamptonshire. Dad christened him "the little watchmaker" but he accumulated four fifties in six innings and topped the Test averages. Steele was voted BBC Sports Personality of the Year as much for courage as achievement but he could not prevent the Test series being lost 1-0, almost a decent result given the previous winter's carnage.

England's best chance of victory came in the Headingley Test, but the last day was abandoned after one part of the pitch had been dug up and another had been soaked with a gallon of crude oil in the middle of the night. The vandalism was committed as part of a campaign to secure the release of George Davis, who had been imprisoned for armed robbery. Australia would have resumed on 220-3, but still needing another 225 to secure the series. That game also saw the Test debut of that graceful slow left-armer Phil Edmonds, who took 5-28 in the first innings. I still have the audio-cassette I made of him dismissing Ross Edwards for a first-ball lbw, playing no shot. It makes bittersweet listening, though, because the commentator is the erudite Alan Gibson, whose drinking got him sacked for good from the *Test Match Special* team on the fourth evening of that game.

The Headingley match was almost as memorable for Dad, who, having endured a week of excruciating pain, had to go to hospital for an operation on the fourth day. All went well and we trooped in to see him on the Tuesday. He was in good form. "I thought when I went under the anaesthetic I'd be able to watch the cricket when I came round and now they've dug the pitch up." He was soon back to his equable best, though. Dad never nursed a grudge for long, even towards the Germans, and they'd tried to blow him to bloody bits.

There were other things about that Australian summer. Even in a tour which began on June 25 and ended on September 3, Ian Chappell's men played 10 first-class games against the counties and one against the MCC. We could follow them round the country. Also, the Sunday of each Test was a rest day. "I need it as much as the players," said a friend.

Already in 1975, I was as bewitched by cricket writing as by the game itself. (Playing proper cricket came later.) On the morning of the first day of the opening Ashes Test, BBC Radio 3 broadcast *The Sound of Cricket* an anthology of music and poetry presented by John Arlott. I treasured my cassette of that programme for nearly 40 years, playing it only rarely for fear that the tape would snap. I had it converted to CD, so now I can listen to Arlott's concluding comments whenever I wish.

"Where lies the last word?" he began. "On cricket there is no last word. It's ancient, yet modern; in some ways, unchanging; in others, constantly in a state of change. Indeed, if it isn't all things to all men, it's different things to most men, for it takes on the character of the period when it's played, the place where it's played and the people who play it."

When I become intolerant of the more extravagant claims made for T20, it's often helpful to remember Arlott's wisdom and prescience that blissful July morning when my world was young. Summer drifted by. While others worshipped Tony Greig, Jeff Thomson or Clive Lloyd, I was reading all I could find by JM Kilburn, Ray Robinson and RC Robertson-Glasgow. And I carried on collecting books with barely a scrap of discrimination. The Venerable Bede never had a chance.

Paul Edwards is a freelance sportswriter who writes regularly on county cricket for ESPNcricinfo.

Clive Lloyd en route to his century in the World Cup final

VIC MARKS

1976

THE LONG, HOT SUMMER OF VIV AND 'CAPPY'

A first sighting of an all-time great and the reappearance of a cricketer carved from granite

---

In 1976 the charts were topped by Queen (with *Bohemian Rhapsody*), ABBA (*Mamma Mia*) and the Wurzels (*Combine Harvester*). *The Fall and Rise of Reggie Perrin* was unmissable on our little TV screens as was *The Sweeney*; Concorde flew and Apple produced their first computer; Jim Callaghan took over as prime minister and, sadly, I was already an adult – more or less (I was still a student) – and a first-class cricketer.

It was the heatwave summer when the outfields were scorched brown by July, the summer of Viv Richards and Michael Holding announcing themselves to the world at large, of the parched Oval packed with joyous West Indian supporters in the final Test of the summer, of Brian Close's England recall, of Ian Botham's England debut (in an ODI against the West Indies at Scarborough

with Alan Knott captaining the side) and, of course, of Oxford University winning the Varsity match at Lord's.

I'm prepared to concede that the last item may have passed you by. But I remember it. The Varsity match was still worthy of note; John Woodcock of *The Times* and most of the other senior correspondents would attend the match and report it and as captain of Oxford it all seemed pretty important to me. The two universities also combined for matches against the tourists and in the 55-overs per side Benson & Hedges Cup.

We played the West Indies at Fenner's, a reminder that in 1976 there were no helmets – they would only become commonplace in 1978 as everyone, except Richards, followed the lead of the Packer players. In that game Peter Roebuck, a Cambridge undergraduate as well as my Somerset colleague, was struck on the head by a delivery from Andy Roberts and forced to retire hurt. This was a serious moment. Batsmen were

Brian Close receives some chin music from Michael Holding at Old Trafford

seldom hit in those helmetless days – though earlier in the summer Dennis Amiss had been hit when playing for the MCC against the West Indies. As a consequence Amiss overhauled his technique and explored how to protect his head. Before long he would emerge in a white motorbike helmet looking like a superannuated Hell's Angel. We giggled, though not for long. This obviously made sense.

It was a different game before the helmet. Batsmen were more wary of hooking because that increased the chances of getting hit; they were also more adept at ducking and weaving. They may even have watched the ball more closely. Tail-enders were far more likely to give themselves a little more room by retreating in the direction of the square-leg umpire. Were they more cowardly then? No. They just recognised the need for self-preservation given that the sole protection available for the head was a cloth cap – though Mike Brearley and Sunil Gavaskar had just begun experimenting with skull caps under their normal headgear.

The beauty of Barnsley in 1976 springs to mind. That is where the Combined Universities played their last zonal B&H fixture. It had been a struggle to cobble together a team as exams were looming and it was a long way from home. Moreover we could not qualify but Yorkshire could if they beat us. Sadly Geoffrey Boycott was not playing in that match but he popped his head into our dressing room to wish us luck.

Yorkshire, despite the presence of Bill Athey, John Hampshire, Chris Old and David Bairstow in their ranks, batted timidly, overly conscious of the looming possibility – and subsequent humiliation – of an unexpected defeat. Out in the field we sensed the eyebrows of the PA man heading north-wards as he announced the introduction of bowlers such as the soon-to-be-ordained AR Wingfield Digby and R le Q Savage at the old home ground of Dickie Bird and Michael Parkinson. We started to enjoy ourselves as Yorkshire crawled to 185-7. Then Gajan Pathmanathan, the mildest of Sri Lankans who was opening the batting with Roebuck, assaulted the bowling of Old, thrashing 58 in no time. We won by seven wickets with eight overs to spare. Boycott popped his head into the dressing room again. "I wished you luck. But not that much luck."

Back at Somerset after the end of the university season our captain had gone missing. Actually we all knew where he was. At the age of 45 Brian Close had been recalled to the England team by Tony Greig in a vain attempt to make the tourists grovel. He did not even bother to put a cloth cap on for protection. He did not possess a chest pad; his thigh pad was wafer thin. After scoring a very respectable number of runs in the first two Tests

(144 at an average of 48) Close was pummelled at Old Trafford by a barrage of short-pitched deliveries from Holding on the third evening. Later Viv Richards would recall whispering out of the corner of his mouth to his county captain (he did not want to be seen by his colleagues to be showing too much sympathy to the opposition): "Cappy, are you alright there, man? Are you OK?". Close told him where to go.

No cricketer of my experience had as much self-belief as Close and how he needed that quality when pitched against the West Indies' ruthless bowling on a dodgy surface. This was the first season in over two decades that he had not put the England fixtures in his diary. He was dropped after the match at Old Trafford and upset about that. He suspected that Greig had left him out because he was worried that he might be superseded as captain – by Close, of course. "Players kept looking at me when I was at short-leg in the Test matches," he would tell us upon his return to Somerset. "So I put 'em in right place."

It was impossible not to revel in the domination of Richards over the English bowlers in that series (829 runs in seven innings). It was no surprise to us at Somerset. After two seasons on the staff with him we knew he was extraordinary – it only took an innings or two to recognise that – and we might have shared this revelation. Now nobody could argue with our assessment. We had been lucky enough to see him first.

Another young teammate, whose subsequent ascent to the pinnacle was not quite so obvious at first glance, was fast maturing as well. At Trent Bridge, Ian Botham hit his maiden century, an unbeaten 167 to win the match for Somerset against Nottinghamshire. He finished with 1,022 first-class runs in the season and 66 wickets. His reward was a forgettable ODI debut in Scarborough in a defeat against the West Indies – his Test debut the following year against the Australians would be more notable.

So 1976? This was the year when confirmation was at hand. Yes, I was privileged to play in the same team as two of the greatest cricketers of all time (three if the inclusion of Close is allowed, four if we can stretch to 1977 and the advent of Joel Garner at Taunton, five for the dedicated 'Demon of Frome' fans). All this plus great unanimity with our European neighbours thanks to the generosity of the decision-makers on the continent: the United Kingdom won the Eurovision Song Contest. It was an awfully long time ago.

Vic Marks is the *Guardian*'s cricket correspondent, a regular contributor to *Test Match Special*, and the author of *Original Spin*, among other works. He played six Tests for England.

ASHLEY GRAY

1976/77

THE AUSTRALIAN CIVIL WAR

As Packer prepared to take on the establishment, Australian cricket staggered into a messy fight for its future

---

The charge of the Hill Brigade was on, though their preferred weapon of attack was not musket rifles but unopened cans of beer. Full-strength lager launched by burly men in singlets and terry towelling bucket hats intent on teaching the ancient SCG scoreboard and its tardy attendants a prompt lesson in mathematics.

Their crime: an inability to keep up with the streaky four-hitting of Gary Cosier, Australia's ginger-haired No.6, who'd had the temerity to edge and square-cut a rampant Imran Khan for four successive boundaries.

As hundreds of aluminium missiles whizzed past cowering spectators towards the hand-cranked scoreboard and its attractive bat and ball weather vane, I comforted myself in the knowledge that my grandfather had chosen a safe viewing position for us on the wooden benches in front of the old Bob Stand, a good 20 metres from the infamous Hill.

In hindsight, the chaos of that opening day of the third Test against Pakistan – so routine it wasn't even reported in the *Sydney Morning Herald* the next day – was almost a portent for the unruly battles that would follow, just months later, for the soul of international cricket.

Watching an entire Test match live is something of a rite of passage for Australian 'country' boys. We'd caught the train down from Newcastle (100 miles north of Sydney) – the hometown of the uber-talented Gary Gilmour and the uber-inconsistent Bob Holland – and booked in to the People's Palace, a cheap and cheerful Salvation Army hostel for working people.

The preceding Christmas I had made the leap from a willow with a 'terry-armoured' coating, which looked like the manufacturer had dipped it in Tippex, to an oil bat, a Gray-Nicolls Record, size 6. 'Signed' by Doug Walters – I'd have preferred Greg Chappell, but snow-blind Saint Nick obviously didn't understand the pecking order of Australian batsmen among young boys – it had signalled my intention, as a 10-year-old, to get serious about making the Test team. Throughout that summer, the grand old Aussie institution of backyard cricket played host to my shiny new Gray-Nics. Its initiation, however, was disastrous: a lusty, bedroom window-shattering square-drive, which gave me a lifelong fear of lofting the ball, even millimetres off the ground.

Attending the Test match was recognition that I'd come of age as a fully-fledged cricket head. I now had a bat that commanded respect, plus I had a soft spot for serial underperformer Kerry O'Keeffe – a sure sign I wasn't a bandwagon fan. It was also a lesson in the perils of hero worship.

In the two previous summers Dennis Lillee and Jeff Thomson had pulverised both England and the West Indies, putting the baggy green on top of the cricket ladder – not that many players from that era of Australian cricket chose to wear one. But cracks had begun to appear. Ian Chappell retired, then Thomson dislocated his shoulder in the first Test, significantly lowering the speed limit of the Aussie pace battery. A sense of stuttering indecision was most apparent to me in the second innings of that match when keeper Rod Marsh, normally as bold and belligerent as his porn star moustache, blocked out the last few overs of the game instead of pushing for victory. Australia fell 23 runs short with four wickets intact.

After the macho, blood-on-the-pitch heroics of 1974/75 and 75/76 the drawn result felt a tad wimpy, almost *unAustralian*. Was Bacchus missing his good mate Chappelli at first slip, commentators speculated? Brother Greg was an astute leader, they said, but no man's man in the same way his elder sibling was.

So it wasn't entirely shocking to see a 23-year-old Imran Khan bag 12-165 in that third Test as Australia slunk to an eight-wicket loss, reducing the likes of Rick McCosker and Gary Gilmour to single figures on a benign track. But to a boy only just into double figures himself, it was Lillee's lion-hearted effort on the final day, when all was lost, that struck a lasting chord. Tasked with picking off 32 to win, Pakistan's openers Majid Khan and Sadiq Mohammad must have thought their first win on Australian soil a mere formality, but Lillee had other ideas. Shirt unbuttoned almost to the navel, his blistering four-over spell was a masterclass in pace bowling, yielding the scalps of Sadiq and Zaheer and scaring several kilos of bejesus out of the portly Mushtaq.

The takeout was crystal: sure, my heroes were completely towelled, but they never gave up. For Australian cricket fans, the summer of 1977 never really ended.

The Pakistani tour was followed by a two-Test visit to New Zealand and the Centenary Test in Melbourne. Save for my torrid backyard contests, this was probably the most serious sporting event in Australia's cricket history up to that point; so serious we were even allowed to listen to the commentary on transistor radios in class. A heart-stopping 45-run victory neatly set up

Greg Chappell's men for the tour of England, which started only a month later.

Set to the inglorious backdrop of Kerry Packer and the ICC's fight for the control of the game, the four-month-long Ashes tour was a shambles from an Aussie viewpoint. The ABC television broadcast, which was a direct lift from the BBC, began at 8pm. Jim Laker's lugubrious tones – matched by the equally lugubrious bowling of Mike Hendrick, whose stock and strike ball were exactly the same – kept me going till the strictly enforced bedtime of 9.30pm.

In his diary of the tour, *The Ashes '77*, Greg Chappell wrote that experience was the difference between the two sides – and he was probably right, but there were also some baffling umpiring decisions to contend with. I can still picture Tony Greig at his smirking best edging a searing Thomson thunderbolt off the shoulder of his bat to Marsh in the second Test at Old Trafford. Then umpire Spencer giving it not out despite the fact that the ball had deviated the width of a small-size cargo ship. Maybe it was because he was unsighted: Greig had quickly pivoted towards gully in an attempt to conceal his misdemeanour.

Cricket's civil war was on in earnest when the 1977/78 summer began just a month after the England campaign ended. On one side was the establishment, led by the side-burned Bobby Simpson, a 41-year-old throwback to the conformity of the 1950s; on the other was World Series Cricket skipper Ian Chappell, all permed hair and bristling 'tache, Marc Bolan to Simpson's Perry Como. Where did my loyalties lie? For a young boy, it was cricket in excelsis: there were now two teams to pledge allegiance to: one stacked with eager to-impress no-names, the other with lofty heroes.

Of course, my grandfather – and a majority of Australians – didn't see it that way. The ACB welcomed Bishan Bedi's Indians and our eagerly anticipated SCG Test tradition continued as if the Packer 'circus' had never happened. But St Nicholas had obviously felt the winds of change. That Christmas I received a WSC Cricketeers membership pack, consisting of an avocado-green supporters cap, a board game, tickets to Country Cup matches (played by the 'Cavaliers', the team reserved for outcasts from the Australian, West Indian and World XIs) a page of facsimiled autographs, and most importantly a flexi disc of *C'mon Aussie C'mon*, the new TV anthem. Packer was already winning the marketing war.

I also discovered my Gray-Nicolls Record was out of date. The old-school maroon, black and white label had given way to a funky, more 70s-friendly, red and light-pink number. This never-ending summer had claimed another unsuspecting victim.

Ashley Gray is an Australian writer and the author of *The Unforgiven* – the story of the West Indian 'Rebel' cricketers who toured South Africa in the Eighties.

Tony Greig and Greg Chappell prepare to toss-up ahead of the Centenary Test

Geoffrey Boycott runs out local favourite Derek Randall at Trent Bridge

JON HOTTEN

1977

THE RETURN OF THE BESPECTACLED MUTINEER

*A distant, mysterious figure stepped out from the shadows
to steal the show*

his is a story about 1977, but it begins the summer before, on August 13, 1976 at The Oval. It was England v West Indies, fifth Test, second morning: my first day of live Test cricket. It was also the summer of a famous drought. The ground seemed vast and brown, blistered and burned by endless sun. I'd watched the first day's play on TV, and West Indies' new star batsman Viv Richards made exactly 200 not out. He went on to get 291. Viv swaggered off slowly, apparently unbothered by his proximity to a triple hundred. Towards the end of the West Indies innings, the group of blokes behind us began to talk about England's opening batsmen and what was going to happen to them. They were sharing a pair of binoculars and arguing over who'd get them. "I want the first ball of Amiss," one said.

I sort of knew what they meant. Clive Lloyd had built a new kind of war machine made of brutal fast bowlers and England were being smashed into submission. Edrich and Brearley had opened in the first Test, Wood and Brearley in the second, Edrich and Close in the third, Woolmer and Steele in the fourth and now it was to be Amiss and Woolmer in the fifth. They survived for the night, but Holding and Roberts were bowling so quickly that the ball, from 90 yards away, was almost invisible.

One name was absent from that list, the name of my dad's favourite player: Geoffrey Boycott. I knew that he was in some kind of exile but I didn't know why. He was a remote figure, written about in the papers, talked about on television. One of the few sportsmen, like Muhammad Ali or Brian Clough, who could reach beyond the back pages. Everyone knew Boycott. People loved him, people hated him, but it was quite hard to actually see him play because the only cricket on television was the Test matches or the John Player Sunday League. He seemed distant and mysterious.

All I had was Geoff Boycott's *Book For Young Cricketers*, in which he outlined his techniques and practice drills, and my dad in my ear, telling me to try and emulate the great man's immaculate defence.

What I didn't understand were the roots of Boycott's exile, the complex mix of external events and internal forces that kept him away for three years. He was 34 years old when he stopped and approaching 37 when he came back.

It was an Ashes summer. Tony Greig had left the England captaincy to join Kerry Packer's World Series Cricket, with Mike Brearley taking his place. Boycott had been the first player to turn Kerry Packer down. On May 14, he met Alec Bedser, the head of selectors, at Watford Gap services. Boycott was worried about being seen by photographers so his return was negotiated in Bedser's white Austin Princess. Bedser left him with the words, "The ball's in your court".

The squad for the first Test had already been picked. That game finished in a draw. Australia played three first-class matches before the second, the last of those against Yorkshire at Scarborough, where Boycott went for nought in the first innings and then made 103 in the second. England won at Old Trafford, but the failure of Dennis Amiss cleared the way. Boycott was back.

When the squad for Trent Bridge was announced, Boycott was joined by another, much newer star of the English game, Derek Randall, who had made 174 in the Centenary Test at the MCG during the winter. Randall had a manic, nervous energy at the crease. He was constantly in motion, pulling at his gear, twitching, gurning, talking to himself. He was probably the best fielder in the world too, running in almost as far as the bowler from his position at cover. And there was a debut for Somerset's Ian Botham, who bowled an astonishing spell on the first day: 4-13 at one point.

But it was Boycott I was waiting to see, and he made sure no one missed him. He batted on all five days of the match, and the redemptive arc of his summer began. At 11, I could have had no idea what it would have meant to him.

Early on the second morning, he ran Randall out and buried his face in his batting gloves. He was dropped on 20 by Rick McCosker. He could have folded but his determination was absolute. By the end of the day he had 88.

"There were people there willing me to get out, the hatred ran very deep," he later said. "Then to run the local hero out.

It would have been the easiest thing in the world to give a slip catch and get off the stage... That was by far my best innings."

He made 107, his 98th first-class hundred, and 80 not out in the second innings, and then went to Edgbaston with Yorkshire the following week and got a hundred there. Ninety-nine centuries, and his next knock at Headingley against Australia in a Test match.

As a kid to whom the world had always been kind, I had no doubt he would do it. I couldn't wait for it to happen. Now, I marvel at the unlikeliness of it all: of life bending itself into the shape of happy-ever-after fiction – and how rarely that happens.

It was like Boycott and the whole of Yorkshire willed it true. He barely slept the night before the game. At three in the morning he ordered tea from the night porter at the hotel. Brearley won the toss and batted. The crowd roared and shivered. Brearley got out third ball. Boycott made 34 in the first session, and another 35 between lunch and tea. He was like a man walking along a high wire, never looking down. My dad was driving home from work early, hoping to see him do it. Geoffrey scored 10 in the first hour after tea. Australia thought they had him caught down the leg-side. My dad got home and we went next door, because our neighbour had come home early to watch it too and he had a bigger TV.

The time was ticking away towards the six o'clock news. Boycott inched through the 90s. By 5.49pm, he was on 96 and facing Greg Chappell. Chappell bowled a floaty, inswinging half-volley and Boycott pumped it down the ground. He tried to raise his hands in the air but they dropped behind his back, the bat dangling from them. People raced onto the ground. Someone stole his cap. He was surrounded but alone.

Standing around the TV, we all cheered. The innings was on the news and in all the papers. It was a water cooler moment long before anyone knew what a water cooler was. The next day he went on to 191 and England won by an innings. Since his comeback, Geoffrey Boycott had batted for 22-and-a-half hours, and I'd watched all of them.

As a kid, you think that this is sport – a thing that exists to fulfil these kinds of storylines. Boycott's feat will never be repeated now. Even the thought of it seems dreamlike, too good to be true.

When you're 11, you can believe in stuff like that.

Jon Hotten is the author of The Meaning of Cricket *among other works and is the reviews editor of* Wisden Cricket Monthly.

PAT MURPHY

1978

ACCESS ALL AREAS AT EDGBASTON

With World Series Cricket into its second year, the impact of Kerry Packer's revolution was being felt in county dressing rooms across the land. Warwickshire's was no exception

The summer of 1978 was hardly a golden summer in the meteorological sense. It rained. Then some more. I can't remember a wetter summer. For those of us harbouring delusions of adequacy on the field of play, it was a miserable season. Fond hopes of that first century, or even a great catch in the outfield, were dashed for yet another year as it simply bucketed down when each weekend approached.

The BBC Midlands team that I captained (qualification: you'd watched the 10 o'clock news at least once) missed eight successive Sunday games. There were two options each Sunday lunchtime; sit in the pub moaning about the fates, or do something constructive. I chose the latter, with significant consequences.

By then, I knew that the best way to forge some sort of a career as a cricket journalist was to get to know the current players on the first-class scene and to win their trust. No less an authority than the great John Arlott had given me that advice when we first met the previous year, and who was I to cavil? If it worked for my broadcasting hero with Hampshire in the 1940s, I would try the same, 30 years later.

I was lucky, though. The Edgbaston ground was just down the road from the BBC's Pebble Mill studios and I would slope off whenever possible. I had also become friends with Bob Willis, after collaborating with him on our first book. *Pace Bowling* was published early in the summer of '78; it was a slim volume, bulked up by excellent photographs and a modicum of insight. It was never going to lead to a new mantelpiece chez Willis or Murphy, to accommodate a clutch of awards, but it opened so many doors for me.

Bob was incredibly generous in broadening my contacts with so many thoughtful introductions. He made it clear I could be trusted. Supping pints with him in the Prince of Wales pub just behind Birmingham's Repertory Theatre constituted the 'imprimatur' in the eyes of his Warwickshire teammates. Soon I was drinking in fresh insights and gossip about the game with David Brown, Neal Abberley, Dennis Amiss, Steve Rouse, Geoff

Dennis Amiss sporting his pioneering new helmet

Humpage, Steve Perryman and a youthful Andy Lloyd. They couldn't have been more helpful. Hopefully they were impressed by my willingness to get the beers in, stoutly denying they were on BBC expenses…

Bob then broadened my knowledge by introducing me to his friends in the England team. A Test match against Pakistan at Edgbaston and another pilgrimage to the Prince of Wales led to meeting Bob Taylor, Geoff Miller, the debutant David Gower and an emerging young talent by the name of Botham. Soon I was ghosting Ian Botham's column in *The Cricketer* magazine. More precisely, in those days when there were no mobile phones, I'd be pestering his wife Kath with countless phone calls to their home, finally grabbing a few minutes with him after a fishing/roistering jaunt and somehow padding out a few random thoughts into a semi-readable column.

A book with the unfailingly professional Bob Taylor on the art of wicketkeeping soon followed and before the season was out he and Gower had agreed to a diary collaboration for the forthcoming England tour to Australia, which the visitors won 5-1. Thank heavens it was such a triumphant tour; subsequent shambolic trips Down Under wouldn't have sold many books!

By now, I could steal into the players' dining room at Edgbaston and watch the action, picking the brains of those who were particularly friendly and willing to deal with my gauche questions. I also spent invaluable time with EJ 'Tiger' Smith. At the time, Tiger was the oldest Test cricketer in the world – 92 years and counting. He had been captained by WG Grace, kept wicket to SF Barnes in an Ashes series, umpired in the 1938 Lord's Test when Wally Hammond scored a majestic 240, and coached Warwickshire to their 1951 Championship title. This man exuded cricket knowledge and history and he had no qualms about sharing such omniscience.

The current Warwickshire players clearly respected him and he thought little of telling Mike Brearley where he was going wrong with his batting technique. I can still see Tiger in that dining room, handing Brearley his walking stick, imagining it was his bat, telling him not to wave it around so much. Brearley, unfailingly polite, knew that a man who had batted with Jack Hobbs, kept wicket behind Victor Trumper and umpired Don Bradman knew a bit about batting. For this novitiate cricket reporter, it was an amazing experience.

I knew there was a great book in Tiger. The deed was done. Two provisos – it wouldn't be published until after his death and I insisted the derisory publisher's advance should go to his loving family. When Tiger passed away in August 1979, I was humbled to find that in his will he had left all his *Wisdens* to me. I am looking at them all now on my shelf as I write this. I remain humbled by that gift, 40 years on. Getting Tiger Smith's approval was the most exacting rite of passage in the summer of '78.

But it wasn't the most harmonious time in that Warwickshire dressing room. Dennis Amiss had signed for Kerry Packer and Bob Willis and David Brown were among the most vociferous

critics of their old friend. Soon Dennis, emboldened by supportive calls from World Series Cricket, had taken up an entrenched position as his teammates stopped talking to him. He decided that the best way to get through this torrid season was simply to occupy the crease as long as possible, compile a stack of runs so that Warwickshire couldn't possibly sack him – and let his teammates moan as much as they wanted. He ended up the only batsman to score 2,000 first-class runs in that rain-ravaged season.

Dennis never needed any second bidding to bat for long periods, but when he was out he'd come into the dining room, chat to myself and Tiger (who had coached him), then write letters on World Series Cricket headed paper, unperturbed that any playing colleague passing by would spot what he was doing. Tiger would tell Dennis he was in the wrong, Dennis would fight his corner, and I'd just sit there, astonished that I was lucky enough to have a ringside seat.

A few months later, Dennis became a key figure in finding a peaceful resolution to the dispute between Kerry Packer and the Establishment. Once Packer was assured that Dennis would be offered a new contract by Warwickshire, a rapprochement was reached. But the heavy lifting was done by John Arlott, David Brown and Jack Bannister of the Professional Cricketers' Association. Dennis had played with Bannister and Brown at Warwickshire and phone negotiations ensued between Austin Robertson for World Series Cricket and Brown and Bannister on behalf of English cricket. I was privy to those phone calls. I lived just a mile from Edgbaston and Brown and Bannister would turn up for late night debriefings, wondering how the eventual peace treaty would play in the media. I had no problem about being sworn to secrecy, I was just overwhelmed to be trusted and fascinated at the fine details involved in the discussions.

A few months later, Dennis got a new contract and both sides claimed victory. I got the exclusive about the imminent breakthrough, aware that Dennis was central to a story that had seismic implications for the game at large. It seemed a long way from those genial chats with Dennis over a beer in the Prince of Wales just a few months previously.

But it wasn't just Edgbaston matters that occupied me. I often popped down to Bristol or Cheltenham to catch up with Brian Brain, that fine veteran seam bowler, who'd now moved down the M5 from Worcestershire to Gloucestershire. The man who began his career bowling to Peter May and eventually ended it trying to dismiss David Gower had a wealth of stories and insights from the county circuit and soon I was writing his monthly column in *The Cricketer*. We got a book out of it a couple of years later (*Another Day, Another Match*), and after Brian paved the way for me to meet his captain, Mike Procter, that friendship led to a couple more books in the ensuing decade. I was learning that the world of county cricket is a small but generous one.

It was also no hardship to breeze into New Road, Worcester, my favourite county ground, to yarn with Basil D'Oliveira, a hero to my generation. Reg Hayter, the editor of *The Cricketer*, was Basil's agent and he kindly arranged an introduction for me. A

couple of pints in the New Road bar at close of play soon led to carousings in other Worcester watering holes and Basil would unburden himself by describing the events of 1968, when he endeared himself to the nation through his dignity.

So another book had its genesis in a pub and *Time To Declare* was published in 1980, when the great man finally retired at the age of 102, or thereabouts. John Arlott wrote the foreword. D'Oliveira and Arlott in a book written by yours truly – I could have packed up my trade there and then, because it was never going to get better than that.

By the time the 1978 summer had squelched to its soggy end, I was on the way to becoming a half-decent cricket journalist. My contacts book was filling up, players were at last returning my phone calls, publishers were expressing mild interest. It proved to be the most significant summer in my career. The prolonged rain, dragging me away from fanciful notions of playing the game tolerably, gave me the time to work on the foundations. I would never be as busy again in a summer. It was all so new. And exciting.

Pat Murphy is a British sportswriter and radio broadcaster who worked for the BBC for 43 years. He has published more than 40 books, including collaborations with Imran Khan, Viv Richards and Graham Gooch.

Bob Willis relaxes in the Edgbaston changing room

MATT THACKER

1979

SUNDAY REMEMBRANCES

The much-loved John Player League shared the spotlight with the World Cup in 1979, both contributing to an unforgettable summer, except for the bits that have drifted from memory

Memories are treacherous creatures. It's early summer 1979, a weekend. Us three boys, 9, 11 and 13, are playing cricket in the garden and our little sister, possibly wilfully, probably obliviously, encroaches onto the 'pitch'. Dom hurls the ball in, possibly wilfully, probably obliviously, and hits her square between the eyes. She goes down in a heap. I can still feel the icy chill engulfing me, whole body in shutdown – we'd done a bad thing, we'd killed her, we were going to have to pay.

Talking to my folks about the incident recently, they had no idea which of us had thrown the ball. Did they just forget, did we close ranks, was the bruising actually so minor that it barely registered?

It's hard to know what's real, what's meaningful. Our unreliable memories adapt to fit the world we inhabit. In 2013 artist AR Hopwood started advertising for 'false' memories that he would turn into artistic representations. Someone who wrote in believed

his girlfriend's sister had died at the dentist and his 'memory' of this meant he kept all his own dental visits a secret.

On the same theme, cognitive psychologist Elizabeth Loftus convinced a quarter of her subjects that they were once lost in a shopping centre as a child and in a similar experiment, carried out by associate professor of Psychology Kimberley Wade, 50 per cent of participants 'remembered' taking a hot air balloon ride as a child when they were shown doctored photographic 'evidence'.

This phenomenon can have serious consequences. Eighteen people in the US have been sentenced to death based on witness testimony before DNA evidence proved them innocent. But mostly, false memories are inconsequential ("I'm sure you had the remote last") and evidence of a healthy brain filling in information gaps.

Sorry, back to 1979. With a warning to treat the veracity of the rest of this piece with caution. It's obviously easier when you have the internet to fall back on, but who says that's accurate?

I know Liverpool won the league (again), that Arsenal beat Man Utd in a brilliant FA Cup final finish, that Trevor Francis won

Notts Forest and Brian Clough the European Cup, that Maggie became PM, and that Sebastian Coe ran a mile in world-record time. And then Lord Mountbatten was blown up by the IRA. But these are all TV, quiz show, sports fan memories. Hammered home through repeated viewing, telling, hearing. World Series Cricket? West Indies wearing pink? Batting helmets? Supertests? There's nothing of these events that I can categorically say I remember.

But John Player League on a Sunday. Now that is clear as day. Snippets, freeze frames, names, anticipation. For us boys it was heaven. Ball games or do-it-yourself *Superstars* in the garden, regularly interrupted with a bit of watching what was happening at Old Trafford, Canterbury, Northampton. And this nine-year-old's heroes? Stuart Turner, John Shepherd, Anton Ferreira, Trevor Jesty, Jim Love, Andy Stovold, Peter Denning, Bernard Reidy, Paddy Clift, Norman Gifford, Ted Hemsley, Graham Barlow. O my Hemsley and my Barlow not that long ago.

Why it was these journeymen and not the more obvious stars I took to I have no idea. I'm sure it says a bit about Englishness and a lot about me, but I don't know what. It's not like the John Player League was short of big-name attractions – England's stars would regularly pull on their county sweater the day after a Test match and then there were the likes of Imran Khan, Javed Miandad, Clive Lloyd, Gordon Greenidge, Clive Rice, Malcolm Marshall, Zaheer Abbas, Richard Hadlee, Mike Procter, Glenn Turner, Ken McEwan, Viv Richards, Joel Garner – this was the golden age of embedded overseas players, two a side and in for the long haul, with the obvious exceptions of Yorkshire and Glamorgan, with the latter, it seemed to me, packing their side with as many Joneses as they could muster.

The BBC coverage (black and white in my mind's eye – not sure if that was the telly or the technology) was introduced by the pipe-smoking Peter West, or Peter Walker, with Jim Laker doing the commentary. There were probably loads of others but I only remember Jim. Stern but warm, he took me through the summer, taught me the rights and wrongs of proper cricket with his gentle admonishments as teams walked off having posted 160 in their 40 overs and knowing they'd probably got enough runs in the bank.

Then it'd be poring over the paper on the Monday – always an extra big sports section on Monday – and scouring each scorecard, assimilating those all-important middle initials that sorted fandom's men from boys, checking on my favourites, watching the table take shape.

And then, for a glorious fortnight in June, the World Cup. I'd been too young in '75 so this was my first. I remember precisely none of the matches leading up to the final. I have no recollection of flags flying as we beat the old enemy on day one, or of dancing in the street when we skittled Canada for 45. But the final, I remember that. It was big, boisterous, brash, blaring and unlike anything I'd ever seen in cricket.

I loved how when England fielded Gower camped on one side and Randall the other – it was as if nothing could ever get through. Randall, lovely ragdoll Randall, ran Greenidge out, then Haynes went, and little Kallicharran and big Clive Lloyd too. But Collis King arrived to play an innings that would not have been out of place 40 years later, but in 1979 was breathtaking for its violence and power.

And to finish the innings, Viv Richards walked across his stumps and slapped Mike Hendrick up and into the stands. Hangdog Hendrick, who I loved watching bowl over after over of maidens, just short of a length, jagging away, missing the outside edge by a foot, smacking into the keeper's gloves. Hendrick, who rarely conceded two an over. Hendrick, who was never hit for six. After that, I knew we'd lost, that a mountainous 280-odd in 60 overs was plenty too many.

As for England's reply, I remember mostly the futility. And my real hero, the dashing Gooch, blazing away gamely, bat periscoping, moustache bristling. (I had a white polyplastic DF too...) And the suddenness of the ending, of stumps all over the place, of thinking how unfair it was that Garner's arm came from over the top of the sightscreen, even though I had no idea what that meant.

Apparently later that summer, India toured. And we won, although Gavaskar nearly chased down 400-and-something at The Oval. Not a single recollection of that entire series. Funny thing, memory.

Matt Thacker is managing editor of *Wisden Cricket Monthly* and the *Nightwatchman*, the Wisden Cricket Quarterly.

Malcolm Marshall in action for Hampshire in the John Player Sunday League

Ian Botham leaves the field after his epic innings at Headingley

TOM HOLLAND

1981

IN THE COURT OF SIR IAN

In the crusade for hearts and minds,
no other summer comes close

hen I was a child, the rhythms of the year were structured for me by my father's love of sport. The moment I heard football scores drifting out from the radio I knew that winter was coming. Anxious mutterings about Aston Villa's relegation prospects meant that the days were lengthening again. Spring would be heralded by the sudden appearance outside our shed of various black metal sheets with white numbers on them, which my father would then lovingly repaint. This, I came to understand, meant that the cricket season was due to arrive. Summer was marked by weekend after weekend when my father would appear dressed in whites, vanish after a hurried lunch, and not return until it was dusk. Then abruptly, one afternoon, Aston Villa would be on the radio again, losing one-nil. And so the years would turn.

I never really paused to consider that my father might listen to football or play cricket out of enjoyment. I assumed he did it for the same reason that adults did all kinds of strange things: because they were adults. I hated sport. I hated playing it, I hated watching it, I hated everything to do with it. This, by the time I was 13, had become an entrenched part of my identity. My brother might enjoy playing cricket, but not me. I was the one who refused to have anything to do with it. It was part of what made me me.

The months that followed my 13th birthday, however, saw my resolve starting to crumble. It was 1981, and the England cricket captain, Ian Botham, was much in the headlines. Even I found it impossible not to be aware of his travails: the series of defeats that he had suffered against the West Indies, his own calamitous lack of form, the likelihood that he was going to lose the Ashes. Whenever he appeared on the news, he had the look of someone who absolutely detested cricket. I began to feel a certain fellow feeling for him. By the time the series against Australia began that summer, I had actively come to identify with his uselessness. His performance in the second Test match, when he made two ducks and got sacked as captain, confirmed me in a surprising realisation: I actually had a sporting hero.

Circumstance then intervened to cement it. My mother had to go into hospital. My father, charged with looking after me during her absence, made what I can now recognise to have been an eminently sensible suggestion: that we sit down and watch the next Test match. Half reluctantly, half in anticipation, I agreed. The first three days, it is fair to say, did not go well. The cricket was dreary and England played appallingly. Only the performance of my new-found hero provided the faintest grounds for optimism: six wickets and a half-century. By the morning of the fourth day, though, I had had enough. John Boorman's new film about King Arthur, *Excalibur*, was on at the local cinema, and I wanted to see that. My father, accepting that England were going to lose, agreed to take me. We went to the matinée. Coming out of the cinema, heading to the car park, driving home, he would occasionally wonder aloud just how badly England had lost. I did not engage. I had given cricket a chance. It had let me down. I was simply not interested in what might have been happening at Headingley.

Excalibur had told the story of a hero emerging out of darkness, of scarcely credible feats, of a legend destined to endure for eternity. So too, that dank July afternoon, did the coverage from Headingley on BBC Two. Every reader of this book will know what my father and I discovered when we switched on the television on our return from the cinema. There is no need for me to rehearse the details of Botham's century, the course of Willis' eight-wicket spell. Suffice it to say that by the end of the Headingley Test I was utterly, hopelessly smitten. Nothing in the world, I had decided, was more exciting than cricket. I had fallen in love with it as I had never fallen in love with anything before.

"Just be warned," my father said sagely. "Test matches aren't always as exciting as that." This turned out to be true enough, of course – but not immediately so. Miracles that summer abounded. Edgbaston followed Headingley; Old Trafford followed Edgbaston. Only when the series arrived at The Oval

did I finally get to watch a match in which Botham did not go berserk, and everything ended up tamely in a draw. By that point, however, I didn't care. Not even England's tour to India that winter, to play a series widely held to have been the most boring of all time, could put me off. The memory of the Test matches I had watched that summer, hallowed by multiple retrospectives in newspapers, magazines and TV programmes, had made me a fan for life.

And not just a fan. A player too. The box full of numbers for the village scoreboard, which my father kept in our shed, were transformed in my mind's eye from enigmatic ciphers into emblems of romance and fascination. A similar alchemy touched the local sports field. No longer did I see it as a place that threatened stultifying boredom. Now, when I heard the clattering of studs on a pavilion floor, smelt freshly mown grass, helped my father to lift up the scoreboard, I felt much like a page might have done at Camelot. If cricket was a wonderful sport to watch, I thought, then how much more wonderful it would surely be to play. So I began practising. There were nets down at the sports field, and my brother and I, for an entire month, would head down to them every morning, balancing our kit precariously on our bikes. Then we took the logical next step: we put a net up in our garden. Admittedly, it was not ideal. The net itself was on a steep slope, and the space for it so cramped that the bowler's run-up was only a couple of steps. But it was serviceable enough. My brother and I played multiple Test matches. We hit an endless number of balls over the wall. I learned to pitch the ball vaguely on the wicket. Before the season ended, I had even managed to play my first match for our local village. I didn't bat, didn't bowl, and dropped a catch – but even so, it felt like a dream come true.

And now, 39 years on, I can see that it was indeed a dream come true. Many improbable things happened during that summer of 1981 – but as improbable as anything, perhaps, is the fact that it brought me to fall in love with cricket. While I feel faintly embarrassed to have chosen such a predictable year for this book, I do not feel apologetic about it. For me, as for so many others, 1981 was the most golden of summers. I am touched by its aureate glow still.

Tom Holland is a writer, historian and Authors CC legend.

ANDY ZALTZMAN

1982

ALL-ROUNDERS OF THE CRICKETPOCALYPSE

A summer in which the whole spectrum of Test cricket was on display

ricket invaded my consciousness over the legendary summer of 1981, which was, by any standards, a more than passable summer in which to be introduced to humanity's greatest creation. By the following season, at the age of seven, I was fully, life-changingly obsessed. My father had given me *Botham Rekindles The Ashes*, the *Telegraph*'s book chronicling the dramas of those six wildly undulating Tests, replete with Bill Frindall's handwritten scorecards and a titillating wodge of introductory statistics. I was hooked. As all right-thinking people in the same circumstances would have been.

The following season was therefore my first complete summer as a cricket fan, the first in which I followed England's Tests from start to finish – India first; then, for three gripping Tests

during the school holidays, Pakistan. If '81 was an almost too-perfect first encounter, '82 provided the ideal exposition of the myriad magnificences of cricket, embedding the game immovably into my soul. It was a season of comic-book-hero allrounders, whirling narratives, noisily trumpeted triumph and defeat, and the realisation that I didn't really care who won. I just loved watching cricket. The Zaltzman family television earned its corn that summer.

Memory, famously, is a trick-playing con artist who cannot be trusted. My recollections of 1981 have been painted over by repeated watchings of highlights videos (although some are genuine and unaltered – Australia's Dirk Wellham being agonisingly wedged on 99 for what seemed like a significant proportion of eternity, before finally reaching a century on debut in the dead final Test at The Oval, was understandably omitted from the BBC's *Botham's*

Ashes video, but I retain a powerful sense of awkward tension whenever I hear his name).

The summer of 1982, however, is etched deep, the Pakistan series especially, when school was over and there was, clearly, nothing to do other than sit on my own watching days and days of Test match cricket.

Objectively, it was one of the most dramatic three-Test series ever played. England won a tight first Test that pivoted on a 79-run 10th-wicket partnership between Bob Taylor and Bob Willis. Pakistan scored a dazzling Lord's victory with only four overs to spare to square the series, after Mudassar Nazar's legendary 6-32 blitztrundle, before England clinched the series with a three-wicket win at Headingley, after collapsing from 168-1 to 199-7 in pursuit of a target of 219. England won 2-1. They almost won 2-0. They could have lost 3-0.

I jotted down my personal memories of the series before referring to the all-knowing archives of the internet. They include, in no order of prominence, relevance or clarity: the mystery and intensity of Abdul Qadir, my first encounter with wrist spin; Graeme Fowler's 86 on the second innings of his debut; plentiful moustaches; Robin Jackman's elongated shuffle to the crease; the bearded, vigorous Imran-esque Tahir Naqqash slicing through the cream of England's batting; Mohsin reaching his double hundred, and the commentators noting that it was the first at Lord's for 33 years, fixing the name of Martin Donnelly in my already stats-curious head; Mohsin being out almost immediately after reaching his double hundred; the wild excitement created by an away win in England, and specifically at Lord's.

I remember the sense that Gatting Would Eventually Succeed (despite the fact that, by the end of that summer, he had a highest score of 59 after 22 Tests). I remember Ehteshamuddin, summoned from league cricket for the decisive final Test, not exactly exuding the honed athleticism of the elite sportsman. He managed 14 overs in the match before physics and physiology conquered him and injury struck. He was a good bowler – 500 first-class wickets at 20, and a Test five-for in India – but to the seven-year-old me, he was an impostor. I remember Botham pinning a Pakistan opener leg before wicket for nought with the first ball of the innings. (It was Mudassar, it was in fact the second ball, and this happened in both innings of the first Test – I am not sure which of these two I am slightly misremembering.)

I also remember actively enjoying the grinding obduracies of Chris Tavaré, my local Kentish hero, batting for hours and hours and hours. He made 54 off 180 balls in the first Test, 82 off 277 in the second, 216 off 734 in the series as a whole. He had already anti-cudgelled 178 runs off 543 balls in the three Tests against India. In all, he batted for almost 30 hours in the two series combined. No one has ever batted longer in an English summer without scoring a century. His personal tally for 1982, expressed as a team score, was 394 all out in 212.5 overs. After Botham, he was my favourite England player. I was an odd child.

The Lord's match has fastened in mind with particular clarity, perhaps because it was my first experience both of watching England lose, and of hearing the distinctive timbre of English commentators when England were doing something awful in a Test match – in this case, losing six batsmen (including Gower and Lamb for ducks) to a medium-paced dobbler who had not taken a Test wicket for two-and-a-half years. It was a tone that would become increasingly familiar as the 1980s unfolded.

There is a decent selection of highlights on YouTube. These jolted further long-buried micro-memories – Derek Pringle's unusual white-grilled blue-bodied helmet; Gunn & Moore bats with a narrow blue-and-green stripe down the back; the controlled majesty of Zaheer Abbas; Ian Greig's bowling action; staggeringly close unhelmeted fielders swarming around the batsman, which allowed Miandad to take a blindingly intimate silly-point catch to dismiss Pringle off Qadir at Lord's.

At the heart of it all, Imran Khan and Botham. Imran was early in the stratospheric peak phase of his career, in which he arguably played Test cricket as well as anyone has ever played Test cricket. At the crushing height of his bowling, between 1980 and 1986, he took 184 wickets at 15.9 in 33 Tests (excluding two matches in which he was unable to bowl, due to injury). From the start of this 1982 series, at which point his career batting average was 25, until his retirement 10 years later, he averaged over 50 with the bat. And he captained his team to numerous landmark results while playing with enough charisma to turn a box of hamsters into a herd of elephants.

Botham, on the other hand, was approaching the end of his sport-expanding pomp. The jaw-dropping feats of cricketing implausibility, such as he had perpetrated in the Mumbai Test of 1980 (probably the greatest individual match performance in Test history), and in the final four Ashes Tests of '81, would become more sporadic, and the unstoppable deluge of wickets had decelerated to a still-impressive flow. At the start of the series, Botham had scored five centuries and six further half-centuries in 20 innings since his captaincy-ending pair at Lord's in 1981, averaging 64 and scoring at 75 runs per hundred balls.

By coincidence, both men would play exactly 48 more Tests after the end of the 1982 series. Imran averaged 51 with the bat and 20 with the ball; Botham's figures were 29 and 37. (By coincidental co-coincidence, the fourth horseman of the unprecedented all-rounder cricketpocalypse, Richard Hadlee, was also 48 Tests from the end of his career; he would average 33 with the bat and 19 with the ball up to his retirement in 1990.)

For this series, though, they were near equals. Imran took 21 wickets at 18, Botham 18 at 26; no other bowler took more than 10. Each man made two half-centuries. Imran had the statistical edge, but Botham ended on the winning side, taking nine wickets and hitting a rapid and important 57 in the decisive Test.

Bob Willis and Imran Khan shake hands after England defeat Pakistan in the first Test Edgbaston

My recall of the Indian half of the summer is more fragmentary, beyond a general sense that Kapil Dev and Botham were, at the time, the pinnacle of humanity. They batted seven times in the series. Botham made 67, 128 and 208 (then the fastest double hundred in Tests); Kapil's innings were 41, 89, 65 and 97. Between them, 695 runs came off 772 balls, with 13 sixes and 86 fours (a boundary every eight balls faced), numbers that would be outlandish even now, and were positively otherworldly then. The other players in the series collectively averaged 33, with a strike-rate of 42, and reached the ropes once every 24 balls.

It was the perfect summer for a young English cricket fan. The entire spectrum of Test cricket was on display, from Kapil's 89 off 55 to Gower's 29 off 152 and whenever-Tavaré-was-at-the-crease. In the final Test, Javed Miandad alone made 54 off 183 and 52 off 57.

There were match-altering tail-end partnerships, as well as scores of 0-2, 9-3, and 45-5. There were collapses, fightbacks, double hundreds, ducks. There was pace, swing, leg-spin, finger-spin, dob, sub-dob and dib-dob. There was umpiring. And angry reactions to umpiring. Heroes excelled. We won. But the opposition were glorious. Five of the six 1982 Man of the Match awards were given to visiting players (and the other to Botham) – Kapil Dev and Sandeep Patil, the highlight of whose Old Trafford century was hitting six boundaries off a seven-ball Bob Willis over, won commemorative Cornhill medallions for India; Imran, twice, and Mohsin, did so for Pakistan.

The cricket had all the brilliance and flaws, successes and struggles, eruptions and longueurs, the collective and individual narratives and subplots, that have fascinated and enraptured its followers since the dawn of international cricket and beyond. It set Kapil alongside Tavaré; Qadir next to Hemmings; Imran beside Ian Greig. Names, faces, styles, numbers, stories, carved into the early memories of a small boy with an overworked television.

Andy Zaltzman is a writer, comedian, host of the satirical comedy podcast *The Bugle* and *Test Match Special*'s resident statistician.

SIMON BARNES

1983

THE YEAR OF THE UNDERDOG

*The third edition of the World Cup saw an unlikely, rousing
triumph that would alter the game's path forever*

e are participants too. Every cricket match that matters to us is our story. It belongs to us just as much as it belongs to the players. Public events are invariably packed with private meaning. The newspaper tells us one narrative while we live another: not parallel but inextricably intertwined.

So it is that great cricketing matches become parables and fables and omens and cautionary tales, each one apparently aimed at an audience of one. This second narrative of the match is all our own, forever mixed up with the disasters and heroics that happened on the pitch.

This, then, was my first English summer for five years: my first summer of cricket since 1978. Alas, the four-match Test series against New Zealand failed to set fire to my imagination in that summer of 1983, for all that England won it 3-1.

I was waiting for the World Cup. Only the third time it had been contested. It was to be held in England for the third time running, for where else could it ever be played?

Though to tell the truth, I was less English than I used to be. That's because I went to India in 1976. I was 24 and the place knocked me clean off my spindle. Two years later I set off to live in Asia – to seek misfortune. I was there four years, living the life of a Gonzo journalist and doing all the mad travelling I could. I lived on Lamma Island, which lies a little to the south of Hong Kong. The final trip of Asian life took me back to India.

So home. Home? Really? Never quite planned that, but there I was, and in the company of a beautiful girl. Could be worse, then. We married and set up in a bedsit in Ealing. I did two days a week at the now defunct *Titbits* magazine, an odd experience but one for which I am forever grateful. I also did shifts on the *Daily Mail* features desk, usually working on the horoscopes. Plus a bit of

Kapil Dev lifts the World Cup trophy alongside Mohinder Amarnath, Player of the Match in the final

work for *The Times*. Life was a little more circumscribed than it had been beneath the Asian sun.

By the time the World Cup came along, I was ready to shout for underdogs and for Asia. Different times, different game: 60-overs each way and only eight teams. They had to play each other twice in the group stages for reasons not entirely unrelated to money. West Indies were more or less guaranteed to win for the third time in a row. Sri Lanka were just making up the numbers and India were no-hopers.

England were great, though. And very confident. They won five of their six matches to reach the semi-finals, finishing top of their group. And they were certs to reach the final. After all, they were drawn against India.

Not that India had played at all badly, but they were perceived as soft. Supine, even. Short on self-belief and too easily downhearted when things went against them. As they did against Zimbabwe. Of all people. Kapil Dev came in with four wickets down for nine, which rapidly became five for 17. He then scored 175 of a total of 266, next highest score 24. Perhaps there was something about this India team after all. I was happy about that. Nothing like a good underdog, after all.

And then India beat England in the semi-finals. I seemed to be supporting both sides at once, though perhaps my patriotism for the nation of Underdog was dominant, certainly by the end. India bowled beautifully on a pitch that suited their seamers of quiet pace, and England could only make 213. That's 213 in 60 overs. (The to-date record for a T20 international, by the way, is 278.)

We had tickets for the final. My father got them and we all went together. I wore a shirt I got made for me in Mysore. West Indies were the inevitable opponents. We heard on the way that West Indies had won the toss and were bowling: we wouldn't even get a decent day's play. We entered the ground to the most terrible groan. Sunil Gavaskar was out for 2. We'd be home in time for tea.

India were bowled out for 183 and it's my firm belief that if they'd made any more they'd have lost. But this was an opponent and a total that West Indies were simply unable to take seriously.

Sometimes sport will take you to a magic land, where unimaginable things happen as a matter of course, when reality is left on the ground as we all go floating up into the clear skies of sporting fantasy. At such times the impossible becomes the inevitable and the merely extraordinary is run-of-the-mill.

The long afternoon unfolded with the mad logic of *Alice Through the Looking-Glass*. Everything was the wrong way round, but it was beyond anyone's power to change it. Everything had to be accepted for what it was: clearly impossible but manifestly true.

The most terrifying batting line-up in cricket history was undone by gentleness. It was like judo, in which the master mysteriously persuades his much bigger opponent to throw himself. The lions were beaten up by the Christians, the sheep rounded up the collie-dogs and the mice made mincemeat of the cat. The flowers spoke, the train leapt a brook and the White Knight won the day.

These things are often a matter of belief, and belief was granted to us all by Kapil Dev, running thousands of yards with his back to the wicket to take a glorious catch and dismiss Viv Richards. One by one they came, one by one they left: the fearsome gentleness of Madan Lal (3-31) and Mohinder Amarnath (3-12) did for the West Indies and changed cricket for ever.

And me, I sat entranced in my Mysore shirt, and it seemed to me a glorious message telling me that all things are possible. You can come from Asia to England as a no-hoper and still – well, with a bit of luck, you could still do all right.

India, it seemed to me, had that bit of luck. We all need that. The important thing is that they didn't take this luck as their due. They accepted it in humility, seized it with deep gratitude and then did all they possibly could to make the most of it. And that is the most useful possible lesson to anyone setting out, however belatedly, however reluctantly on the road that leads to the land of the grown-ups.

Simon Barnes is a novelist, journalist and birdwatcher who was chief sportswriter at *The Times* until 2014. His most recent novel is *The Game's Gone* – about a sportswriter.

TANYA ALDRED

1984

THE MAROON-BLAZERED GALÁCTICOS

The world-beating West Indies, endless garden cricket and bubble-bath Winston Davis beards

It was May 1984 – the beginning of my last summer of primary school. Days passed in a haze of handstands and the fear of imminent nuclear war, and televised sport played very little part at all.

But then a crack commando unit arrived at Heathrow. They wore smart maroon blazers and open-necked shirts and were lithe, debonair and quite brilliant. They leant casually against the wall and demolished England's cricketing straw-hat. An entire tour slipped by from mid-May to mid-August and they lost only one match – a one-day international at Trent Bridge – and as for the Test series, well, 5-0 was polite.

They didn't look like those other sportsmen, often just a Cornish pasty away from elasticated trousers. These guys laughed as they sprang in the air to pluck the juicy red apple from the sky, they high-fived as yet another hundred clocked in, bowled long-limbed Exocets, and topped it all with a rolling strut to win the heart of any pre-teen with taste.

England had endured a dismal winter – becoming the first English team to be beaten by Pakistan and New Zealand, hampered by both injury and accusations of pot smoking. Few thought that the summer would reverse the last three series defeats by the West Indies, and any optimism lasted until, oooh, the first one-day international at Old Trafford when Viv Richards in West Indies cap and Rasta wristband, cocked Duncan Fearnley in his hand, calmly struck one of the greatest one-day hundreds.

His 189 not out included a six into Warwick Road station leaving England's bowlers scuffing the dust and the delighted crowd sprawling out onto all the pavilion balconies. And so it would continue for the remainder of the tour, barring that

Joel Garner bowls
to Paul Terry,
batting with a
broken arm at
Old Trafford

West Indies fans celebrate their team's 5–0 win over England

sketchy and unconvincing win by England at Trent Bridge – which was immediately followed by a resumption of normal service, and another Richards exhibition, at Lord's.

"I have always felt as a black man that there are so many unfair people out there," Richards later said. "I wanted to show them that we can climb the mountain too." The mountain was duly climbed.

We watched a lot of the series on our grandmother's television, a relic even in 1984, which belched when switched on and, in a branch of physics still undiscovered, squashed the picture from the top down. This didn't render the West Indies any less omnipotent.

From the first match against Worcestershire to the joyous celebration of blackwash at The Oval, West Indies were a team first, just one bulging with individual talents. There was Viv, of course, and Gordon Greenidge, and Roger Harper with his origami arms and Velcro hands and Michael Holding coming off his long run at The Oval and most memorably of all, Malcolm Marshall, at Headingley, playing on with a double fracture of the left thumb. He batted to allow Larry Gomes to complete his century, thrashed a one-armed boundary, then, hand in plaster, beguiled figures of 7-53, his compact little body so fast, so perfect. And in charge of all these blades, Clive Lloyd, a man who at times resembled a weary old dog shuffling off for one last walk, but who held it all together.

There were moments of English dominance – especially at Lord's, where they were on top until the innings of the summer, 214 not out from Greenidge, led to Gower becoming the first England captain since 1948 to declare in the second innings and lose. Allan Lamb was the rare creature able to counter-attack the West Indies squadron of fast bowlers, with three centuries (only Graeme Fowler made another) and Ian Botham took his 300th wicket. Other than that, the highlight of each Test was the relief that followed when Richards was out.

In between the fourth and the fifth Tests, my dad took my three brothers and me up to Lord's, to see West Indies play Middlesex. It rained for most of the day but we discovered Joel Garner signing autographs as he perched on the steps of the tour bus, his extendable legs stretched out in front of him, a real life BFG. Cricket's allure had by then soaked through our pastel coloured windcheaters. In the bath, my brothers patted bubbly Winston Davis beards into place. We collected the Texaco Trophy caricature cigarette cards – which slotted pleasingly into a green paper folder. And after school the early evening highlights became routine viewing.

My parents had bought an old house with a big garden the previous year – and all summer we were outside. When my brother Sam was forced to wear a sling after an insect bite became infected he became a perfect stand-in for Paul Terry, who, left arm broken trying to avoid a ball from Winston Davis at Old Trafford, came out to help England save the follow-on. And amid scenes of confusion, had to face Garner with his arm in plaster. My middle brother Toby protected his head from a barrage of tennis balls with his CHIPS (Californian Highway Patrol) helmet that he had unwrapped the previous Christmas. It wasn't actually a bad homage to the head protection England were hiding behind.

The summer ended with a one-off Test against Sri Lanka which was supposed to provide light relief but ended in further humiliation. Gower invited the Sri Lankans to bat, and had to watch them do so for two days with centuries from Sidath Wettimuny and Duleep Mendis. Only the ever-reliable Lamb scraped much dignity from the situation; England were even booed by the Lord's crowd for slow scoring on the Saturday afternoon.

That West Indies side of 1984 was unbeatable in a way that must be unimaginable to children who follow cricket today. They were the All Blacks and Real Madrid combined – with the same fear and excitement but more grace, perhaps more joy, and certainly fewer financial endorsements. It was both political and awesome. What I didn't realise as a child, was that these men were all-time greats, at their all-time prime. What luck, to stumble on them that long hot summer.

Tanya Aldred is a freelance writer and editor, co-editor of the *Nightwatchman*, the Wisden Cricket Quarterly, and a creative writing teacher for children.

DANIEL
NORCROSS

1985

LESSONS IN LOVE

*An Ashes-winning summer when our man was struck by multiple arrows
from Cupid's bow, delivered from inside and outside the boundary*

Not only had I just turned 16 in the Ashes summer of 1985, but by a curious quirk of my single-sex schooling I was in the first of what would be three years in the sixth form. The Sixth Form. After years of confinement in class, rote learning for a million useless O-Levels, I finally had 'Free Periods'. Delicious dollops of liberty, often in the afternoons, when you could slip out of school, chug on a fag in Dulwich Woods, and dream hopelessly romantic thoughts (perhaps that's being kind on myself) about any number of girls from our 'sister' school, James Allen.

No longer would I have to catch surreptitious updates on *Test Match Special* via a 'tinnie trannie' (a potentially ambiguous and offensive phrase now, but one that was then used to describe a portable radio with impossibly bad reception) using the hinged lid of a battered school desk to provide cover, while pretending to search for my Latin primer. It was the 1980s so I could instead brazenly pop to the pub unchallenged to watch whole hours of cricket.

England's Test team was in pretty good shape going into that summer. They'd pulled off a surprising victory in India without Ian Botham and with a double century from Graeme Fowler, one of a number of players to benefit from the scandalous rebel tour to South Africa in 1981/82 which had robbed the country of, among others, Graham Gooch, John Emburey, Peter Willey, Arnie Sidebottom and Les Taylor. With their three-year bans now served, all of them would appear at various points during the 1985 Ashes series. Fowler would not.

And Botham was back. It was impossible not to adore Botham, even though this year he sported a diabolical mullet, replete with highlights, and was determined to commit some of the worst

Richard Ellison
took 17 wickets at
10.88 in the 1985
Ashes series

atrocities against fashion imaginable. He seemed perpetually tethered to his sinister agent, Tim Hudson; a quintessential product of that undignified decade of greed, he was himself no stranger to gaudily striped jackets, badly tailored white trousers and grey Hush Puppies.

I was eight years old when Botham made his debut in my first cognisant Ashes summer of 1977. He announced himself with a five-for. We won the series 3-0. Then there was 1981. In between there had been the glorious marmalisation of a weakened Australia in 1978/79. The only Ashes blip had been in the previous series Down Under when we had in turn been shorn of our better players, so in truth I'd led a charmed life. Yes, we always lost to the West Indies but everybody did because they were the greatest sports team ever to bestride the universe. But Botham was back. The traitorous but prolific Gooch was back. An inexperienced Australia was back and I had all the time in the world.

The summer had started well for me. I had wangled the part of Garcin in *Huis Clos* (or *In Camera*), Jean-Paul Sartre's gloomy existentialist musing on the hatefulness of humanity. This allowed me to rehearse and re-rehearse a scene with Jessica, the current object of my affections, in which I had to kiss her passionately in front of Josie who had rejected me some weeks before. Gloomy existentialism had never been so much fun.

And when I got to spit out the line, "Hell? Hell is other people", revenge over rejection was never more complete; in my mind at least. And that is, after all, the point of existentialism isn't it?

Things went well with Jessica for a couple of weeks until I was dumped two hours after England's loss in the second Texaco Trophy match thanks to a match-winning 85 not out from Allan Border which sealed the one-day series for the tourists. How much Border was to blame for Jessica's change of heart I have never been entirely sure, but she has been synesthetically associated in my mind with the gritty left-hander ever since.

Naturally I was devastated for a couple of days but a dalliance with Camilla at a party on the same day that David Gower stroked a velvety 102 in an eight-wicket crushing of the Aussies in the third and final match restored my confidence that this really could be the Summer of Daniel.

All went well initially. Camilla and I canoodled intermittently through a resounding victory in the first Test at Leeds, despite a most unwelcome hundred from the usually fallible Andrew Hilditch. England, though, had found the next Herbert Sutcliffe in Tim Robinson, whose 175 formed the backbone of a massive first-innings total of 533 and despite minor scares on the last day, they eased to victory by five wickets.

Disaster struck at Lord's, however. A combination of the comically-aged leggie Bob Holland, who skittled England's tail with 5-68 in the second innings, and my, on reflection, catastrophic suggestion that Camilla might want to get a perm like Tim Robinson's saw me once more single and the series tied at one apiece.

What followed both on and off the pitch was a period of stalemate. I had become enamoured of Viola. A girl who was wedded to her dungarees, she nevertheless indulged a modicum of cricket chat. As captain of the school second XI I seized my opportunity and suggested she might want to come and see me in action as I demonstrated the erogenous powers of leadership and cunning for which my captaincy was world-renowned.

It was the last match of the school season. Determined to demonstrate that whatever the failings of the pitch, a truly great captain can still conjure wickets from thin air, I put myself in at short-leg after making it very clear to both the batsman and, I assumed, the rapturously watching Viola that I had "seen something" in the opposition's well-set No.3's technique that made him susceptible to our highly erratic part-time off-spinner.

Viola was indeed watching, but only at the point when, emerging from her book, she heard an agonised high-pitch scream as I crumpled to the floor having worn a fierce pull shot on my unprotected nethers. We remained friends, Viola and I, but the crushing humiliation made it prudent to shake hands on a draw at almost the exact same moment that the third Test ended in similar fashion. A truly forgettable match was enlivened only by Gower's sublime 166. Frankly any pitch on which Graeme Wood and Greg Ritchie score large hundreds was never going to bring a result.

The fourth Test was ruined by rain but a pattern of English dominance with the bat was starting to emerge; this time it was Gatting getting in on the act with 160. Australia, with Geoff Lawson off colour and Simon O'Donnell as the third seamer, held no terrors. It has been rare indeed to relish the sight of England batting during my 51 years on this earth, safe in the knowledge that they will pile up runs. Many out there will never have been so blessed, but I tell you, it bolsters your confidence. You become Superman. Suddenly you can do anything.

Off the back of England's 595-5 at Edgbaston – featuring a double hundred from Gower, 148 from Robinson, an unbeaten century from Gatting and a seven-ball 18 from Botham that contained two sixes (one of them off his first ball) and was described at the time by Frank Keating as the greatest innings he had ever seen – I agreed to play the part of Barador, an ageing wizard, in the worst film ever made. A fantasy drivel enterprise penned by my 16-year-old chum Ed who had spent too much time playing *Dungeons & Dragons*. With the working title *Dawn of the Equinoxe* (he was also a Jean- Michel Jarre fan), I had to deliver such lines as, "We must break the necromancy of Sarak and free Zia. For that we travel to the planes of the Aesvaarn". But I didn't care. There were two girls from an entirely different school in it and they were a smidgen older than me. And England were scoring runs like I'd never seen before. Every boundary that Gower smote with effortless ease through the covers just made me more desirable. And right now I was Sting, Robert Redford and George Michael rolled into one.

Filming ended just in time for me to attend every ball of the sixth and final Test at The Oval. For the second match running Gower was involved in a triple-century second-wicket partnership, this time with Gooch. It was a day like no other. Temperatures in the low 80s. Runs coming at four an over. The voluminously spectacled Murray Bennett, looking oddly like snooker world champion Dennis Taylor and bowling roughly as well as him. The certainty that England had the Ashes in the bag.

There was the comedown on day two, with an unnecessary collapse that left England disappointed with their 464, but we needn't have worried. The Aussies were a spent force. Botham took two of the most miraculous slip catches I have ever seen, standing in his alpha male position five yards further forward than was strictly speaking necessary, and England romped home by an innings.

By the end of the series Richard Ellison and Les Taylor were the support seamers for Botham, a development that no one saw coming at the start of the summer. Indeed, it was Ellison, with his own rather meatier perm than Robinson and an epic moustache to match, that stole my heart. I'd known about him. I'd seen glimpses of him in 40-over games on the telly. I'd heard great things about how he was faster than he looked. How he had subtle variations, hidden depths. He could move the ball late and was more than handy with the bat, but only when I watched him with my own eyes did I appreciate that he was the missing piece of England's jigsaw.

That Monday night there was time for one final party before school started all over again. To my immense surprise I fell in love with Cassie. Properly in love. I'd seen her around but we'd never really spoken. That night we talked about our shared loathing of Cecil Rhodes, Andy Peebles and The Hollies. I never once mentioned Wilfred, Ian or Eric. She waxed lyrical over Elizabeth Fry and I never brought up CB. And I never asked her to get a perm like Richard Ellison's. We made it all the way through the winter and into spring before Patrick Patterson et al put paid to the illusion of England's batting prowess. The writing was on the wall.

Defeat at home to India was the final nail in the coffin for both us and Richard Ellison, who would never play a Test match again. But for one glorious (late) summer I was on top of the world.

All names of girlfriends have been sympathetically changed to spare them from association with the author.

Daniel Norcross is a commentator for BBC's *Test Match Special* and has written for *Wisden Cricket Monthly* and *ESPNcricinfo*, among other publications.

Mike Gatting's only two wins as England's Test captain came on the 1986/87 Ashes tour

ANTHONY
MCGOWAN

1986/87

TWO TRIALS DOWN
UNDER

*As Mike Gatting's England side touched down in Australia in 1986,
there was much more on the line for our author than the Ashes*

In the winter of 1986/87 both the England cricket team and my genitals were in a seriously bad way. England had been thrashed in the West Indies the year before, and then well beaten by India and New Zealand at home. Each defeat seemed to hammer home the point that England, despite the egos and the reputations, just weren't very good at cricket.

My undercarriage was in an equally poor condition. Much like Ian Botham, my right testicle was heavy, bloated, and fringed with an unattractive mullet, the colour of a nicotine-stained finger. For the great all-rounder, the unsightly swelling was an effect of an enforced layoff, following his admission of having smoked a joint or three back in his youth. In my case, it was cancer, diagnosed as I lay naked and shivering on a hard marble slab at Manchester Royal Infirmary.

An Ashes tour loomed for England, and an appointment with the surgeon for me. The press gave England little hope of avoiding further humiliation. Martin Johnson wrote famously that there were only three things wrong with the team selected: they couldn't bat, they couldn't bowl and they couldn't field. The news I'd had after my diagnosis wasn't good. Of the various forms of testicular cancer available to the selectors, I'd ended up with the worst. Survival rates were in the low teens – the sort of average you might get from a No.9 batter who could hang around for a while, but isn't going to win you the Ashes. Had Johnson commented on my prospects, I suspect he'd have been equally damning. "There's only three things wrong with McGowan's gonads..."

England were captained by Mike Gatting. I'd always wanted to like Gatting. I admired his pugnacity and could see that back then his fabled flab wasn't, well, flabby, but solid as a melon.

On the other hand, there was that voice, hesitant and high, as if he were answering questions from his proctologist, mid probe. The rest of the team were past it (Botham, Gower, Lamb, Dilley, Emburey, Edmonds) or untried (Small, DeFreitas). Of the two keepers selected for the tour, one, Bruce French, couldn't bat and the other, Jack Richards, couldn't keep. The likely openers were Chris Broad, who had shown some promise, but stuck his arse out in a way that offended anyone interested in the aesthetics of the game, and Bill Athey, who was like a Boycott stripped of the flamboyance.

So, hopes were not high, for England or for me. Post-op, I recuperated at my parents' house in a small, unlovely town in Yorkshire. I'd played since my teens for the local team, then in the Leeds League. It had been my life for a decade, and I still came home to play every weekend from uni. I was a run-of-the-mill club player, opening the batting, usually averaging in the mid-20s. With my long hair, and red neckerchief, I was tolerated as a dandy in a team full of miners and truck drivers and warehouse workers. And now I lay in my old bunk bed, using the cricket to take my mind off mortality, off the cancerous cells I imagined dispersing to all parts of my body, like the field spreading after the first couple of biffs from a Botham onslaught.

The Australians were favourites, but that was more to do with England's perceived weakness than their own strength. True, they had in Border a fine batsman who, perhaps of all the great players, had made the most of what talent he had. But the rest of the team was undistinguished. Marsh was gritty, but boring. Boon had not yet become the rock: at present he was just a fat man with a big moustache, who only moved his feet when there was a lager waiting for him at the bar.

Of the bowlers, McDermott and Lawson were triers, but neither was fully fit. Merv Hughes looked like a fast bowler until he started to run when, with his pot belly and shuffling, flat-footed steps, he looked like he was dashing for the outside dunny after a bad prawn. Only Bruce Reid was genuinely threatening, a quick left-armer with a nasty bouncer. But Australia's recent tour of India had drained him, and now his scrawny figure looked like a collection of elbows and ankles held together by catgut. On the other hand, Steve Waugh was beginning to break through, and Dean Jones had been heroic in India. Jones had the lean and haunted look of an Appalachian cannibal, caught with a collection of gnawed heads in the icebox. He was to be the leading run-scorer in the series.

I had a small radio, with a mono-earpiece, and each night I'd listen to the commentary. Sometimes, when the demons threatened, I'd stay with it all the way through to the next morning. But more usually I'd listen through to lunch. This wasn't due to a lack of dedication, but more because I wanted to watch the highlights the next evening, without knowing what had happened. Who were the TMS commentators? Johnners, of course, although I was never especially fond of his style. CMJ. Blowers. A couple of irritated Aussies. I can't quite remember...

But what I do recall is the rapture, the glory of that first Test, at Brisbane. England had been predictably poor in the warm-ups. There's an amusing story about a heavily hungover Botham going out to bat, his arms swinging in that guess-how-far-I'm-going-to-hit-you way, only to find out, as he tried to take guard, that he'd forgotten his bat. Broad was out early, and it seemed that the tour would die and shrivel in the heat of that first morning.

Gower had been batting at three for the past few years, and Gatting at five, but in one of several brave and astute moves, Gatting flipped their positions, and went in first drop. It was perhaps the best thing he did all tour. With Athey, he put on a hundred partnership, and the tour was saved. Lamb made 40 (his only real contribution in the entire series), Gower a fluent half-century. But this was all the overture. Botham blasted 138, hooking and driving Hughes, and pummelling every other bowler. It was his last hundred for England.

Dilley took five wickets in the Australian first innings, and Emburey five in the second, and England won at a canter. After that, the tour was a doddle. There were hundreds for Broad, Gower and Richards in the drawn second Test. Another Broad century, and one for Gatting in the third. The Ashes were decided in the fourth, at Melbourne. Somehow Botham snaffled five wickets with his medium-paced induckers and long hops, and Gladstone Small's accuracy and movement five more. Emburey and Edmonds, who bowled beautifully all tour, wrapped things up in the second innings, after Broad's third hundred in three games. It was all achieved without fuss, the England team operating for the first time in years as a single organism, with all the parts in harmony. There was plenty of boozing and carousing on the tour, but somehow this generated a centripetal, rather than centrifugal force, binding the squad closer together, rather than ripping it apart, as it had done the winter before in the West Indies.

The Australians scraped a win in the final Test, which probably saved Border's job. The team went on to achieve great things under him. But for England, bad luck, bad management, and age meant that the team was soon broken up.

Looking at the tour averages, it's hard to trace in them England's dominance. Broad and Gower's numbers are impressive, and Gatting averaged a healthy 44. But Botham hardly scored a run after his first mighty knock. Small took 12 wickets at 15, but the other bowlers were taking their wickets at 30-plus, apart from DeFreitas, who had nine at almost 50 (which is a travesty, as he bowled well). For the Australians, Jones scored over 500 runs at 57, and five other batters averaged over 40. But England won all the key moments, each of those vital individual duels that determine the outcome of this beautiful, complex team game.

I'd followed the tour with a dedication to match England's own. And, like Botham and Gatting, it was to be my own swansong as a cricket obsessive. I never again cared so much about a series. When England next won the Ashes, in 2005, I was delighted, but my happiness was superficial. Back in 1987, I'd felt that my fate really did depend on Botham and Gower and Gatting and the rest of the boys.

As it happened, a new family of drugs had been developed that could zap the cancer. The wounds healed. I played for another couple of seasons for the local team, but then drifted to London, and away from the game.

But still, in repose I think of Botham and his absurd mullet, and of Gatting's high-pitched whine and jutting beard; of Gower's grace, and Gladstone Small's neckless brilliance, and Edmonds' flight, and Athey's grit, and of how they kept me alive in the winter of 1986.

Anthony McGowan is an English author of books for children, teenagers and adults. He won the 2020 Carnegie Medal for *Lark*.

The team celebrates Ashes success

ELEANOR
OLDROYD

1987

A WOMAN IN A MAN'S WORLD

*The trailblazing BBC broadcaster recalls an idyllic summer
on the Shropshire beat*

Think of 1987, and what do you remember? England's defeat to Australia in the World Cup final? Mike Gatting's finger-pointing contest with Shakoor Rana? Javed Miandad's epic 260 at The Oval, perhaps?

My golden summer was taking place far from Eden Gardens, Faisalabad, or even Kennington. Instead, I was driving a Ford Cortina Estate with the manoeuvrability of a Chieftain tank, and a radio mast stuck through the middle of it, around the cricket grounds of Shrewsbury, Wellington and Bridgnorth.

Shropshire is a county blessed with natural splendours, from the lakes of the north, to the hills of the south, the narrow lanes of the Welsh borders in the west, to the heart of the industrial revolution in the east. You'd be stretched to call it a sporting

hotbed, though. Life on the BBC Radio Shropshire sports desk in the late 80s revolved around the latest hot goings-on at Shrewsbury Town, the Telford Tigers ice hockey team and, in the summer, Shropshire CCC.

"There can't be many professions around these days that haven't been invaded by women," I wrote in the November 1987 edition of *Minor Counties Quarterly*. "You get women doctors, women company directors, women lorry drivers – but comparatively few women cricket journalists, and even fewer women local radio reporters on Minor Counties cricket. But I don't like to think of myself as a freak – more as a novelty."

In truth, at my highly academic girls' school, I probably was a bit of a freak. A former classmate I bumped into at a school reunion recalled me walking around the playing fields with a thick yellow book in my hand. I would skip German conversation lessons to watch Oxford University playing the

Eleanor Oldroyd on the road for the BBC

Thanks to Eleanor Oldroyd for the photo

counties in the Parks. To get me a day off to go to Lord's to watch the Ashes in 1977, my father wrote to my headmistress: "Eleanor has expressed the desire to be the first woman cricket correspondent of *The Times*, so I feel this would be an educational visit."

The idea hadn't actually crossed my mind until then, but from that point my teenage ambitions were simple: find someone who would pay me to watch cricket all day.

Ten years later, mission accomplished, even if I wasn't rubbing shoulders with the stars. There were no celebrity ex-county pros at Shropshire that year, but former England internationals Graham Roope and Barry Wood turned out for Berkshire and Cheshire respectively. The most high-profile Salopians of the time were golfers Ian Woosnam and Sandy Lyle, and of course the flame-haired Carol Decker of T'Pau, topping the charts with *China in Your Hand*.

But many of the 1987 Shropshire team, including captain John Foster, wicketkeeper Derek Ashley and opening batsman Steve Johnson, had joined former Glamorgan legend Malcolm Nash and Pakistan's Mushtaq Mohammad in a glorious moment for any Minor Counties side – a NatWest Trophy first round win over the professionals. In 1984 they beat Yorkshire at St George's in Telford, with the prized scalp of Geoffrey Boycott taken, caught and bowled, by Brian Perry, a man who defined stalwart; multiple Player of the Year at his club, Wem, and longstanding groundsman at Gay Meadow, then home of Shrewsbury Town.

When Brian died in 2017, I was in Australia for the Ashes and Boycott was part of the TMS team. I was asked if I could get him to record a tribute to Brian, which he did – Geoffrey famously remembers every dismissal of his career – although somehow he managed to make it all about him and his little-known Shropshire roots, and didn't mention the words 'Brian' or 'Perry' at all.

Rewind to 1987, when Shropshire won only two of their nine Championship games, finishing seventh out of the 10 teams in the Western Division. The structure of the competition didn't help anyone, really. Contriving to get a result in a two-day, four-innings game always depended on a generous declaration by one side, and a willingness to chase a total by the other. But at Wellington one July evening, I witnessed the most nail-biting finish to a cricket match I would see until 2019, and the World Cup final at Lord's.

Shropshire needed six to win off the last ball to beat Dorset. Tailender Andy Barnard was the man facing; I stood watching with my *Shropshire Star* colleague and friend Roy Williams, and doyen of Minor Counties reporting, Mike Berry. "If 'Barney' hits this for six, I'm taking off my trousers, shinning up the sightscreen and down the other side," rashly promised Mike. Inevitably, up the ball went, over the bowler's head, over mid-on and over the boundary rope. Somehow we forgot to hold Mike to his pledge.

It was less about thrilling finishes though, and more about the sheer joy of watching cricket of a decent standard, in congenial company, at some scenic spots. A neat pavilion, plenty of space around the boundary to place a deckchair, and a screen of trees to park the radio car beneath. I managed to wangle some away games, too, in my own first car, a bright yellow VW Polo, whizzing down the motorways to Chippenham, Kidmore End or Dorchester, to the accompaniment of Level 42 or the Pet Shop Boys on the cassette player. I remember an idyllic visit to Colwyn Bay in 1988, Wales' first season in the Championship, a sun-washed, cloudless seaside day with the red-roofed houses of Rhos-on-Sea fringing the ground.

No press room to hide away in, no mobile phones, just the radio car or a pay phone on the ground for live reports. Pottering around the edge of the field, occasionally chatting to the players as they waited to bat. And carrying my trusty reel-to-reel Uher tape-recorder for post-play interviews, which were frequently disrupted by laddish banter from the non-interviewees. I got used to it, and the Shropshire players got used to me, but that wasn't the case with all visiting teams, as my piece in *Minor Counties Quarterly* elaborated: "Once I've explained that I'm not there to make the tea or look vaguely decorative on the boundary, the questions start. Most of them begin: 'I don't want to sound sexist, but...' At one match last year I was asked, 'But do you actually write the reports yourself?'" But the biggest FAQ, for years, was: "What's it like to be a woman in a man's world?" Looking back now, I would say: complicated.

The 'invasion' of sports journalism by women was in its relatively early days, and by daring to step away from the tea tent I was stepping, inadvertently, into a sexual minefield. Lascivious comments that would be beyond the pale in this more enlightened era were a hazard of the job back then; I got very good at playing a straight bat at suggestive remarks, perfecting the art of the smiling, ego-protecting put-down. I learnt a lot in those early days about gaining trust and respect from players and backroom staff, and not allowing the boundaries between personal and professional to blend.

But the most important lesson was to be someone people like working with. When, in 1988, I departed for the bright lights of London, captain John Foster made a touching speech, saying how much they'd enjoyed having me around, and wishing me well for my new job at Radio One. It's one of the nicest tributes I've ever had. Many years, and many global sporting events later, I still feel that a small portion of my heart remains in the radio car, on a sunny afternoon on the boundary edge at Shrewsbury, Wellington or Bridgnorth.

Eleanor Oldroyd is a broadcaster with BBC Radio. She co-hosts BBC Radio 5 Live's *Saturday Breakfast* and has twice been named the Sports Journalists' Association Broadcast Presenter of the Year, in 2014 and 2016.

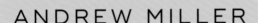

ANDREW MILLER

1989

THE WARM BLANKET OF DEFEAT

England's humbling in the 1989 Ashes series provided an early lesson in managing expectations

At approximately 10.59pm, at the end of a manic Monday in September 2005, I rushed to a bar somewhere in the bowels of Charing Cross, to fulfil a decade-long promise with a group of my oldest friends.

It had been a day of Ashes mayhem at The Oval. The return of the urn and all the hoopla that entailed, and by the time I had dashed off my final piece and legged it to make last orders, Andrew Flintoff and chums were already several hours into the most heroic bender in sporting history.

Back on my parallel timeline, however, the mood took an unexpectedly sombre turn. Sure, we broached our champagne and toasted the end to Australian oppression, but I remember making a conscious effort to bottle the feeling for posterity, and immediately wishing I hadn't. Because what do you do when

all your Christmases come at once? Is this how lottery winners feel when all their existential woes – that daily struggle for subsistence that actually turns out to be your life – are tipped upside down by the mother of all jackpots?

For it occurred to me in the small hours, as I ambled towards the night bus to clear my addled head, that an Australian boot stamping on an England face, forever, had been the comforting constant by which I had calibrated my internal monologue. That thrum of perpetual disillusionment, like a diet of boiled cabbage, had kept my soul more nourished than I could ever have known. And now, like a discombobulated Ossi after the fall of the Berlin Wall, I found myself yearning for a simpler time with simpler implications. I wasn't remotely ready for liberation, for flag-waving, for the tearing-down of monoliths that had defined my very existence.

To be clear, I wasn't unaware that this was a very good problem to have. As an Army Brat, my childhood had been itinerant but privileged – a life spent flitting between Germany and the UK on two-yearly postings, with 10 years of elite boarding school offering a very upper-crust definition of continuity. But a regime of cross-country runs and dormitory bog-flushings was scant preparation for this. Australia's defeat felt like the death of some scabby family cat, the sort that is forever sinking its teeth into your toes in the dead of night, and hisses when you take too long to feed it, but somehow you still miss the savage little bastard when it's gone.

And rather like that hypothetical cat, I can't remember exactly when cricket first dug its claws into me, but I can certainly remember the first time it truly hurt.

The optimism, the misery. The expectation, the self-flagellation. The purposeless churn of right-arm medium pacers, and the Sisyphean clatter of Steve Waugh's endlessly vertical bat. Yes, my sporting awakening had come as an 11-year-old in 1989, of all the godforsaken summers. It was the ultimate kill-or-cure immersion, and I emerged with a soul-deep contamination.

Which details would you care to dwell on for the purposes of this recap? The impregnability of Geoff Marsh and Mark Taylor at the top of Australia's order? The mighty Graham Gooch toppling like a felled oak towards point as Terry Alderman extracted another lbw from his massively planted front pad? Ian Botham galumphing down the track to be stumped for a duck off Trevor Hohns? The flaxen-haired fallibility of a besieged David Gower, forever a theatre ticket short of a competitive team?

Or how about a crash course in politically-charged hero-crushing – aka, "Mummy, who's Nelson Mandela?", as I distinctly recall asking (on a walk through an Oxfordshire graveyard, oddly enough). Neil Foster and Paul Jarvis could have been contenders in my impressionable mind's eye, instead both were expunged from the narrative with the finality of criminals – their mug-shots, along with a cast of other familiars and not-so familiars, paraded on the pale-blue backdrop of the BBC *News at Six*, where previously only disasters such as Challenger or Zeebrugge had truly commanded my attention.

But the truest oddity of 1989 is that I barely saw a single ball. Instead, the series inveigled its way into my conscience over the course of an elongated summer, and as it did so, it time-stamped my awakening as a sentient pre-teen. One minute my memories had been a soup of childhood snapshots – some jumbled, others crystal-clear, but all of them indefinable. Now, thanks to cricket's mental scaffolding that still, to this day, is my *aide memoire*, I can tell you with absolute clarity where I was on almost any given day of that year.

I know I'd been aware of cricket's rhythms since at least the 1986/87 Ashes (note to the Hundred organisers – Daddles the Duck is a gateway drug of a cartoon character). But I also remember feeling slightly non-plussed when, in what must have been May 1988, Graeme Hick's 405 not out against

Worcestershire was reported, to a chorus of squeaky cheers, midway through our school lunch break. Who? What? When? My scouring of the *The Times*' county scorecards clearly wasn't yet up to scratch.

But this time, like some eureka moment in a previously unfathomable algebra class, it all made proper sense. As the summer term kicked in, and my obsessive hours in the nets earned me a first-change berth in the third XI colts team, the onset of the Ashes supplanted the collection of *Garbage Pail Kids* and the covert playing of arcade games on the school's brand-new BBC Archimedes as the only talk of the corridors – or at least, the only frequency I was bothered about picking up.

Headingley and Lord's were my term-time scene-setters. This was the education that my parents had truly signed me up for, as – in the absence of TV or radio – a month of classroom chatter provided the cricket hothousing I needed to get fully up to speed.

I remember how the faux-memories of a decade of Ashes glory had created an assumption of easy dominance among my educators. The legend of Botham, injured at this stage, but ready to ride to the rescue… you wait! The might of the three Gs – Gatting, Gooch and Gower, indisputably at the peak of their powers… you'll see! The pugnacity of Robin Smith, the new buzz-name of the summer, whose early form assuaged the disappointment of two thumping defeats, and whose square-cut was already more awesome than He-Man's!

But before long, as the realisation began to creep that something was seriously amiss, we turned for solace to the creation of our own scorecards. Endless games of dice cricket in Mr McCrae's form room (specifically *Owzthat*, for those who know) would pit the conniving Aussies against teams of global tyrants, just so that 'Healy c Hitler b Pol Pot 0' could be a thing.

And then, suddenly, I was out on my own – spirited back to the drab teutonic stylings of Bergen-Hohne Garrison in West Germany, as the summer holidays began and my separation anxiety kicked in. Somehow I extrapolated enough news from the front line, thanks to intermittent sports bulletins on the World Service, and the once-a-week treat of *Grandstand* on BFBS, the single-channel station that beamed a medley of terrestrial offerings to their ex-pat audience, mostly drippy soap operas and bone-dry documentaries.

Fortunately my own struggles to keep up were matched by the nation as a whole, as 29 players whizzed through England's revolving doors like extras in a Buster Keaton slapstick. I recall musing on the heroism of Jack Russell's Old Trafford century while walking the dog round a fishing lake, and wondering who the hell Nick Cook was, as fleeting footage flashed by of David Boon dumping him through midwicket to reclaim the Ashes.

And having spent most of the month imagining a shared Scottish ancestry with Angus Fraser (the donning of a kilt for a family wedding had sent my sense of dislocated patriotism into a somewhat manic overdrive), I finally saw him bowl – with that high-reaching, hard-toiling, permanently exhausted gait

– and realised I'd found the hero that none of my peers would have been looking for in the first place. A fortnight later, now on a family holiday in Yugoslavia, I harangued my parents to buy a rare copy of the *Daily Mail* to catch up on the action at Trent Bridge, and there, in the midst of yet more carnage, were Fraser's magnificently futile figures of 52.3-18-108-2. If he wasn't going to give up in the face of overwhelming odds, then I sure as hell wouldn't either.

And so the pattern of my adolescence was set, as I grew year on year, but my fandom remained reassuringly stunted by England's biennial inadequacies.

I remember burgling a glimpse of Mark Waugh being bowled for 99 by Phil Tufnell before an English literature class in 1993. I remember telling my parents in 1994/95, no, I don't want to come skiing thanks, I'd rather eat toast into the wee hours and curse at Graeme Hick for not getting a bloody move on. In 1997, I was backpacking through Africa and turned on the hostel TV in Malawi to see Graham Thorpe drop Matthew Elliott at Headingley. I was pushing on through the night ahead of a hotel breakfast shift in 1998/99 when Michael Slater survived *that* run-out at Sydney.

So many scars – even a physical one, courtesy of a headbutted desk in 2002/03, when Craig White drove to gully on the final day at Brisbane. And now, in 2005, so much triumphalism – open-top bus parades, and Johnny-come-latelys dancing in Trafalgar Square's fountains, as if the previous 16 years had never happened. Not for me. Give me misery, give me penury. Give me mismatched logo-less helmets and techniques hewn from a lightning-stricken elm tree. Give me the courage to believe that, next time, it will be different, but the knowledge to embrace that cruel and encroaching strangulation of hope.

Just don't give me what I want, because way back in the mists of time, when this dumb obsession began, I had no idea what I needed. I was just happy to come along for the bumpiest ride I could find.

Andrew Miller is UK editor of *ESPNcricinfo*, columnist for *Wisden Cricket Monthly* and former editor of *The Cricketer*.

David Boon leads the Australian celebrations

Devon Malcolm and Allan Lamb during the first Test against New Zealand at Trent Bridge

LAWRENCE
BOOTH

1990

LOVE, LOSS AND ALLAN LAMB

*An Essex archetype and a precocious Mumbaikar captured the spirit
of the year of the bat*

I t was a summer of small seams, big runs and a French kiss. Wonderfully, it was a time before the internet. It meant my cricket awakening passed in a blur of Tony Lewis and the BBC, Ceefax circa page 340, and two-day-old newspapers from our campsite shop in Provence. You had to make an effort to keep up, and I volunteered for the morning croissant run more than once, rifling through the back pages as I fumbled for francs. God, it was rewarding.

A couple of months earlier, England had toured the Caribbean, losing 2-1 to West Indies in a series they might easily have won. I had fallen under the spell of *Test Match Special* – and Allan Lamb. Cutting and hooking giant fast bowlers from somewhere between the peak of his helmet and the top of his moustache, Lamb persuaded me that

Northamptonshire, his county, would be my county too. Since England's top seven also boasted Wayne Larkins, Rob Bailey and David Capel, it was clear I had chosen one of the domestic game's traditional powerhouses…

So when the 1990 home Test summer began with failure for my new hero (Lamb lbw b Hadlee 0), I steeled myself for disappointments to come. It was only a game. None of it mattered. The real world doesn't give a damn about runs or wickets. Even today, it feels like a useful lesson, especially where Northamptonshire are concerned.

The New Zealand series wasn't up to much, though England won 1-0, which was rare enough in those days. Oh, and Hadlee took a wicket with his final ball in Tests – Devon Malcolm. It was like Shakespeare signing off with "The End". I was happy just to have seen him at work before he retired. Even so, I was secretly hoping that things would get better against India.

Most people remember the first Test at Lord's for Graham Gooch's 333, when the BBC missed the big moment – England's first triple-century for 25 years – because they wanted to show a horse race. But the outrage felt by my 15-year-old self at their priorities was nothing compared with a more personal sense of injustice: Lamb had made 139, yet all the talk was of Gooch and his triple. Fair enough, I suppose. But that didn't make it right.

England ended up winning a lovely game. Mohammad Azharuddin made a sparkling hundred, Kapil Dev saved the follow-on by hitting Eddie Hemmings for four successive sixes into the building site at the Nursery End, Gooch scored another century in his summer of summers, and Lamb was brilliantly caught in the second innings by a young Sachin Tendulkar, stooping low at long-off to take the ball one-handed. Damn him. We'd have to keep an eye on Sachin Tendulkar.

For me, though, matters did not properly hot up until the family holiday in the south of France. We caught the ferry, drove through most of the night, and woke up by the edge of a farmer's field somewhere in the Auvergne, my two brothers and I crammed into the back and grumpily wondering why we weren't nearly there yet.

Once we arrived, the tranquillity of our sylvan surrounds wasn't immediately appreciated. The walk from our pitch to the lone shop would normally have been long enough to put off a tetchy teenager, but the overpriced copies of the British newspapers were my only way of staying in touch with news of the second Test at Old Trafford.

We three boys received a holiday allowance from our parents. My brothers bought sweets, chocolates, tennis balls and snorkels. I bought out-of-date copies of the *Daily Telegraph*, which the whole family proceeded to read anyway. It was worth it, even as I watched my brothers benefit from both their money and mine. Some prices were worth paying.

The game was probably already over as I excitedly returned to the family tent one morning brandishing news of Lamb's almost entirely irrelevant second-innings hundred. No matter that the first-innings hundreds by Gooch, Mike Atherton and Robin Smith had already battered India's bowlers into submission. Lamb now had two centuries in two Tests – and, counting the Caribbean, four in his last nine. His average, I noted after a quick calculation on the back of the newspaper, was now exactly 37. Greatness wasn't necessarily beckoning, but this was a basis for negotiation. And it was higher than Mike Gatting.

Tendulkar saved the Test, announcing himself with a precocious hundred, but my attention was starting to waver.

In the table-tennis room, across the swimming pool, and over the pots and pans I inevitably found myself washing up after lukewarm meals of beans and sausages, a French girl had caught my eye. Miraculously, I seemed to have caught hers.

Her name was Aurelie (don't worry, she'll never read this), and she cared little for the favouritism shown to Gooch over Lamb; she hadn't even heard of Northamptonshire. In fact, cricket may not have featured much at all. I was a latecomer to girls, being shy and at a boy's school. It was my first kiss. And England just needed to avoid defeat at The Oval to secure the series.

All things considered, I was in a good state of mind. I was learning unexpected French words on a daily basis, and found a newspaper which revealed that Lamb had led Northamptonshire to a one-run win in the semi-final of the NatWest Trophy over Mark Nicholas' Hampshire. Since they had beaten Worcestershire in the quarters by four runs, with a fuming Ian Botham stranded at the non-striker's end while Mark Robinson delivered the perfect final over, they were plainly determined to do it the hard way.

Though the supply of newspapers proved sketchy over the next few days, it was clear by the time we left Provence that England were in trouble. In fact, they were following on (Lamb b Kapil Dev 7). My final rendezvous with Aurelie had ended in humiliation, after her father and brother rumbled us in a secluded thicket. The entente cordiale was officially over. But there was no time to brood: England were fighting for their lives.

News of their progress depended on being able to tune into any genre of British radio station as we drove north through France. Finally, not far from Calais, came news that David Gower had saved England's bacon with an unbeaten 157, aided and abetted by Lamb's 52. On the ferry, we sat next to a pair of Scrabble-playing cricket-lovers who hadn't heard the news. "Good for Gower," said one. He seemed genuinely happy.

That summer wasn't just special because England won, I found love, Lamb scored runs and Northamptonshire reached the NatWest final (where they were scuppered by September dew and Phillip DeFreitas). It was a reminder, now I think about it, that summer holidays back then really could take you to another world, with no wifi to keep you in thrall to your own. And the memories feel the sharper for it.

I miss them, those innocent times. I wonder if my French *amie* feels the same.

Lawrence Booth is editor of the *Wisden Almanack* and a cricket writer for the *Daily Mail*.

DEREK PRINGLE

1991

A REGAL SUMMER

A first Test match victory over the West Indies on home soil for 22 years, a Championship title and an impromptu afternoon tea with the Queen

A year before the Queen proclaimed her *annus horribilis* I enjoyed my favourite 12 months as a cricketer, though I don't think the two were connected.

To call 1991 my *annus mirabilis* would be going too far but it was a good season on two counts: England drew the Test series against the West Indies, in which I was involved, and Essex won the County Championship – the former a much rarer event than the latter, at least back then.

The year did not begin promisingly. Towards the end of the 1990 season I'd picked up an injury to my left thigh which I couldn't shake off despite resting at home in Cambridge until Christmas. Usually I spent my winters abroad either playing cricket or travelling, but not this time. I decided I needed to get the problem sorted, though the reality of that

was not straightforward. I had no job, no car and no means of specialised treatment given Essex did not employ players or physios during the winter.

Fortunately, salvation was at hand in the shape of an old school friend, Chris, and his wife Mandy. Although they lived in Wanstead, both worked in The City so barely used one of their cars let alone the second one, a red Peugeot. Generously, they let me use it until sponsored cars began to be dispensed by Essex at the start of the new season.

Mobile at last, in early January I travelled to see Jim Davis, the Middlesex physio, who had a clinic near Harrow. Rest had not sorted the problem so Jim explored the possibility that the cause might be neural, linking it to compacted nerves in my back. About half a dozen sessions with him and the near-impossible exercises he advocated seemed to do the trick.

Derek Pringle
(second left) and his
teammates toast
England's victory
over West Indies at
Headingley

In truth I'd been feeling sorry for myself holed up at home with only *Twin Peaks* for distraction, so the relief I felt at cracking the problem also renewed my enthusiasm to get back into the England side. For the next few months I eschewed alcohol during the week and trained at Fenner's almost every day. In a skill-based game like cricket I'd always been sceptical of the adage that 'hard work brings its rewards', but it did this time. I began the season strongly with bat and ball, well enough to impress Graham Gooch, who was captain of England as well as Essex. With his blessing, no doubt, I was picked for the one-day internationals against the West Indies.

England had a good one-day side in those days and we won 3-0. I didn't have a standout series, though I was denied a hat-trick by some bizarre umpiring from Dickie Bird in the second match at Old Trafford. West Indies were getting well behind the run-rate so I knew that some big shots were coming. My ball to counter that was a slower one which gripped, and which was doubly effective on bare pitches like the one in Manchester. It

worked a treat with both Gus Logie and then Malcolm Marshall falling to skied catches off successive balls. Which brought in Gordon Greenidge, batting at seven due to a niggle he'd sustained while fielding.

Back then, one of cricket's verities was that few batsmen were as dangerous as a limping Greenidge, and here he was so hobbled as to require a runner. Somehow, I sensed he would try to launch his first ball into the crowd so I went with cross-seam fast (at least as fast as I could muster) and straight, to try to get it to skid-on to him. I'd guessed right. He had an almighty smear to leg, missed the ball, and was plumb in front, lbw. Everyone near the pitch appealed, though in truth it felt a formality. An international hat-trick – 'Whoopeee doo,' I thought.

Unfortunately, Dickie Bird had other ideas and gave it not out, claiming Greenidge had hit it. With no Snicko or Decision Review System I had nothing but incredulity with which to win a reversal, though Dickie, much like Margaret Thatcher, was not for turning despite my entreaties.

In 1988 England had also beaten the West Indies in a one-day series, many of the performances influencing selection for the Test team. It was why I got picked that year for the five-day stuff, though at the first sign of a setback the selectors jettisoned me.

I was trying to point out the frustrations of this when interviewed by Peter Hayter of the *Mail on Sunday*. Hayter asked me if I should be selected for the Tests again after our clean sweep in the one-dayers. I told him: "Well, I wouldn't pick me if I was an England selector." Happily, they didn't listen to me and a week later there I was back in the Test side, readying myself once more to take on arguably the most potent team in cricket history.

The first Test was at Headingley and it was unseasonably cold, which helped us as the West Indies' much-vaunted fast bowlers just couldn't get properly loose. Even so, it was a tricky pitch and they were still a handful, but then so were we. Getting some swing and bounce, I managed to dismiss Viv Richards (always the most-prized scalp) caught at first slip, Allan Lamb making up for having dropped him off me the previous evening.

In that match Gooch played what many consider to be the greatest Test knock ever, when he made an unbeaten 154 in England's second innings. It was not a stroke-fest, but on a surface where there were only three other scores above 50, it was definitely a thing of wonder. Writing in the *Sunday Times*, Robin Marlar said its value was "beyond rubies".

Inspired by Gooch's bravura, courage and sheer cussedness, I managed to stay at the crease with him almost two-and-a-half hours to add 98 runs for the seventh wicket. My contribution was a modest 27 but the stand enabled us to leave the West Indies 278 to win, a total that proved well beyond them and we won by 115 runs. Incredibly, it was the first time since 1969 that England had beaten the West Indies in a home Test.

It was also the first Test to be played in England with no rest day, so the match finished on a Monday. To celebrate our rare win, the Test and County Cricket Board – the forerunner to the ECB – allowed us an extra night in the team hotel, a remote place stuck on a moor above Otley called Chevin Lodge. Only four of us stayed: me, Michael Atherton, Steve Watkin and Robin Smith. The evening didn't fizz. Leeds on a Monday night in 1991 was beyond resuscitation. Anyway, it didn't feel right with two thirds of the team having gone home.

We kept our lead when the next Test at Lord's was drawn after the entire fourth day was rained out. That was also the day the Queen was due to meet both teams. With it tipping down, she didn't come. Instead, once play had been called off for the day, both sides were invited to Buckingham Palace for tea.

It proved an enlightening experience, with Her Royal Highness showing a supremely human touch when she met Alf Gooch, Goochie's dad. Alf, who had come to Lord's to pick up his son and drive him home, got swept into the tea invitation. When he explained to Her Majesty that his wife wouldn't believe where he'd been, she went and cut a slice of cake, wrapped it in a serviette with the Palace's coat of arms on it, and said to Alf: "Take her this. She will have to believe you then."

We lost the next two Tests but won the last at The Oval to square the series. I missed that match after falling ill the night before, though I might not have played anyway. Ian Botham had come back into the squad after injury and his competitive instinct was still intact even if, in the words of BBC *Test Match Special*'s Jonathan Agnew, "he couldn't quite get his leg over" after treading on his stumps. The comment sent Brian Johnston into a fit of giggles on air and Agnew's celebrity was sealed.

Essex won the County Championship after beating Middlesex in the last match of the season, which we needed to win. It was our first title under Gooch's exclusive captaincy and there were nerves but only because Middlesex had been bowled out for 51 after being put into bat and we feared the pitch inspector's wrath. As ever, Gooch calmed matters by going out and belting 259 as we put 566-6 on the board. We then bowled Middlesex out a second time, Neil Foster taking 10 wickets in the match, me five.

Other seasons might have brought me more runs and wickets but none gave me as much fulfilment. As Mahatma Gandhi once said: "Satisfaction lies in the effort, not the attainment." In that golden summer, there were both.

Derek Pringle played 30 Tests and 44 ODIs for England between 1982 and 1992. He spent the entirety of his career at Essex, winning five County Championships, before moving into journalism, as cricket correspondent for the *Independent* and then the *Telegraph*, and most recently as a columnist for the *Cricket Paper*. His memoir *Pushing the Boundaries* was shortlisted for The Telegraph Sports Book Awards in 2019.

FIRDOSE
MOONDA

1992/93

CONFLICTS OF ALLEGIANCE

South Africa's readmission into the international sporting fold was by no means a cause for universal celebration, especially in the country itself

et's hope they get a hiding here."

"*They don't know what's coming. They think we can't play cricket. These guys will show them.*"

It was the summer of 1992/93. I was five years old, yet old enough to register the comments being passed around my parents' lounge. Some came from my father, a human-rights campaigner who was involved with the African National Congress. Some came from my two uncles, not as active but just as angry with the injustices of our country's Apartheid policies. All three were cricketers in their day; all played for teams under the umbrella of the South African Cricket Board – the non-white body of administration – and, when the national team took on India in the first home series in 22 years, all of them wanted to see the national team lose.

Though not yet a democracy, South Africa had already been allowed back into international sport. The unity between the white and non-white boards was celebrated globally but seen as nothing more than short-change in our home. We understood it as the more powerful white administration swallowing its non-white counterpart and spitting out its players instead of including them in the new structures. The team that travelled to India the year before was a case in point: it was all-white.

For my father, uncles and many thousands more of their generation, the national team was elitist and exclusionary, a farce that they would not be part of. Instead, they supported the opposition, an easy choice in this case because our family traces its lineage to Ahmedabad in India. We already had a connection to Mohammad Azharuddin's men, and more so to Azharuddin himself. Our family is Muslim and the captain was the only Muslim in the side. In later tours I would discover a deeper connection to Pakistan but for that summer, I remember we were desperate to see India humiliate South Africa.

Jimmy Cook and
Andrew Hudson walk
out at Durban in South
Africa's first home Test
for 22 years

I don't have many memories of the actual cricket. I knew that there was a young player called Sachin Tendulkar that everyone was interested in, that there was a spinner called Anil Kumble, who my uncles were sure would expose South Africa's ineptitude against the turning ball, and that of all the South Africans we disliked, Omar Henry was the one we hated most. He had crossed over and gone to play for the white side in the bad old days. He was what we considered a sell-out.

The only thing I remember vividly was that when Jimmy Cook was dismissed for a first-ball duck, it was as though freedom itself had been obtained. The lounge erupted in noise, there was high-fiving all around and I spontaneously began singing *Nkosi Sikelel' iAfrika*. It was not the South African national anthem then and my dad had religiously taught me the full version. At the end, I used to yell 'Viva Mandela' three times, which became 'Viva Kapil Dev, Viva Tendulkar, Viva India' that day.

A decade-and-a-half later, I was working as a part-time cricket scorer while studying and had become a regular at provincial and franchise matches at the Wanderers in Johannesburg. In the Gauteng team was a batsman called Stephen Cook. He was polite and well-spoken and we became friends.

Almost another decade after that, I was among those who wrote strongly that Cook should be included in the South Africa Test team after seven summers of serious run-scoring for the Lions. When Cook was selected, I felt privately triumphant, more so when he thanked me for being one of the people who had, in his words, supported his case. When he scored a century on debut, I felt vindicated. When he scored two more, after an ugly lean patch in Australia, I felt relieved. When he was dropped for the final Test in New Zealand in 2017, I felt wronged.

The journalist in me didn't want to feel any of those things, even though I can see it as something of deeper significance. Twenty-five years ago, my father and uncles had been so wounded by a system that had denied them that they wished for nothing more than for Jimmy Cook to fail. Twenty-five years later, the system had changed to the point where I could wish for his son to succeed.

South Africa's transformation is far from complete, and has only recently attained the emphasis my father and his ilk wanted to see put on it. The 2015/16 summer was the first time the national team had been required to have more than half the playing XI "of colour". Over the course of a season, CSA demanded at least six players of colour, including two black Africans on average in the team, and they exceeded that. Among the players who made regular appearances were Kagiso Rabada and Temba Bavuma – players no one could argue did not deserve their place in their side.

Also among them was Keshav Maharaj, for whom the India 'Friendship Tour' also had lasting effects. Keshav was even younger than I was then, and his father, Athmanand, like mine, used to play board cricket. Athmanand played for Natal and Keshav grew up in a close-knit community of people of Indian origin in Durban, the first stop of the tour.

The community there made the Indian team feel like they were playing at home, and not just in the stadium. After hours, they opened their homes to the tourists, complete with sumptuously cooked curries and company. At one of those gatherings, Keshav met Kiran More, who looked at his hands and predicted he would become a wicketkeeper. He wasn't too far off – he turned out to be a spinner. Today, Keshav is living his father's dream. I interviewed Athmanand when Keshav was first selected to play for South Africa, ahead of the tour to Australia in November 2016. After we went through the usual stuff about memories of Keshav as a child and stories of how he rose through the ranks, I asked Athmanand how he'd felt about the South African team in the early years of readmission (on a suspicion he shared the views of my family) and whether anything had changed now. His answer touched me.

"Back then we were hurt, because after all the years when we were treated so badly, we also felt as though we were deliberately sidelined afterwards. So, yes, I supported the Indian team then. But now, we can see things are starting to change and even though my roots are Indian and I will always want to see them do well, my son has found a place playing for South Africa and I support him and his team first."

My family's experience is different – they were more aggressively political and the closest they come to international sport is through me, a reporter – so I can't expect them to feel the same way. Not yet. They still say things like, "If Hashim Amla does well and South Africa lose, that would be perfect".

Soon that could become: "If Hashim Amla and Keshav Maharaj and Kagiso Rabada and Temba Bavuma and JP Duminy and Andile Phehlukwayo and Tabraiz Shamsi and Lungi Ngidi do well and South Africa still lose..."

Unlikely, isn't it? And maybe that's when things will really change for people of my parents' generation. Though they remain wronged, their children and grandchildren and great grandchildren for generations to come could experience right. That's the South Africa we all dream of.

Firdose Moonda is a Durban-born writer-journalist and *ESPNcricinfo*'s South Africa correspondent.

PHIL WALKER

1993

RUN-OUTS, BREAK-UPS AND WELL-MEANING CLUELESSNESS

The chaotic summer of '93 breathed new life into the old game and set the tone for the rest of the decade

y folks split up for good in 1993. It had been coming, and then it came, and truly it was a relief; we could all start playing shots again. Cricket didn't save me that year, because I didn't need saving. But it sure kept me occupied. I was 13, old enough to recognise something of love but not so old that it had yet come to dominate – that'd kick in around 15 – and my love back then was for cricket, and cricket alone. I played it, talked it, dressed it, endorsed it, watched it and dreamt it, and because I'd gotten to be quite good – little wonder, Malcolm Gladwell would say – that spring I'd joined a renowned club, one that would make itself limitless in light of love's postponement down Rothesay Avenue.

There were two pitches, a spanking clubhouse and an endless run of conifers separating us from the devil's crossroads at Gallows Corner. There were legions of daft men and giggles of stoic women. There were Essex youth team players in all the age groups. There were Derek 'n' Clive tapes for away games, liberal barmen in the clubhouse, bent coppers in the twos and confused glances at girls everywhere.

The club I joined that summer grafted me to a unit that, through nobody's fault, had been shaken back home. Maybe that's mawkish – if I can't be sure of the actual events any more, I can at least be true to the impressions those facts left. One thing I can be sure of: both provided early, salty versions of *adulthood*, embedding in me a fascination with the shambolic, well-meaning cluelessness of grown-ups which endures all the more now I am one.

Cluelessness was all the rage in '93. This was England, doing cricket, in Waugh time. The game on telly was evolving fast, with Sky Sports revealing just how inept England's winter tours were, and it was in the slipstream of a particularly grim effort to survive India – which, despite knowing the one-sided score, I'd caught large retrospective chunks of on a bunch of videotapes done by my uncle – that the Aussies rocked up for my first proper Ashes series.

It's a magically unspoilt time, being on the cusp of adolescence but not quite there yet. Like running at speed through a dense illuminating forest, before a gap in the trees propels you across a dual carriageway.

And so of that series I remember the lot. The early tour scrap for the opener's spot between two unknowns called Hayden and Slater, and instinctively rooting for Slater; Robin Smith's back-foot straight six off a Paul Reiffel yorker during his 167 in the second ODI at Edgbaston. My first coach at Essex, Peter Such, getting a Test cap and six wickets in the first innings at Old Trafford, binding me personally to what I was seeing. Being in my dad's car listening to the radio when this Warne curio bowled his first ball, *that* ball, and hearing Trevor Bailey exclaim it, "An *ab-sol-ute* CORKER!"

Later that day I got home to see it. I'd been too young for Qadir in the Eighties, and of course there was no English context for it, so this was literally the first time I'd seen such a thing. I toyed with the thought that my man Gower, criminally ghosted by the stiffs and fated to drift away that autumn with an elegiac hundred at a desolate Chelmsford, an innings witnessed by me and Micky Stewart and no one else, would have tucked it away for a couple.

The lot. David Boon's adidas batting trainers. Mark Waugh's multi-coloured bat grip, upturned collar, top button, sleeveless sweater, white sweatband, floppy sunhat, leg glance. Gooch punching one off his stumps at Old Trafford. Nasser's pull shots at Trent Bridge in his Essex lid. Thorpe's debut hundred, lobbing a top-edged hook over Slater's head. Devon Malcolm scorching the earth at The Oval. Border and Waugh (S) batting without heart for weeks at Leeds.

Michael Atherton's run out.

Michael Atherton's run out. I've seen a lot of cricket since that Sunday in July in 1993. This is still the worst.

It's Lord's, second Test. England 0 Australia 1. Second innings, England following on. I didn't yet know about futile rearguards, I just believed in things. Michael Atherton is on 97. He'd made

80 in the first. Border bowls, left-arm over. Michael Atherton clips it into the outfield. Merv Hughes runs around. They run one. They run a second. Hughes gathers. Michael Atherton, 25, turns for a third, but his partner, a barrel of thirtysomething called Mike Gatting, can't see it. Michael Atherton is sent back. He turns. Wrong shoes. He's got the wrong shoes on. He slips. Slips over. He tries to get up, slips again. He's got the wrong shoes on. Hateful Healy, the one with the arse, gathers the half volley, and Michael Atherton is run out.

It didn't change my life, Michael Atherton's run out. It just made me understand it a bit more.

We would all survive that summer. By September Michael Atherton was captain, ushering in a new period of shimmering English dominance with a resurgent victory at The Oval, while back in the real world, my club teams – under 15s, under 16s, and the now legendary Gidea Park & Romford Fourth XI – won everything in sight.

I'd found my place. I'd got a nickname – 'Siggers' – after Sigmund Freud because, you know, I was *dead* clever. I'd got runs and wickets, and made my first hundred for Essex under 13s, in the rain at Buckinghamshire, wafting one through the covers to bring it up. There would be no last-ditch slip in the wrong shoes for me. I guess some of us just have what it takes.

My mum, no great fan of balls, had this knack of being around when I did well at sport, and that day in High Wycombe was one of them. The very next day, we all drove to Devon – me, my little sister, my mate Irf, and my mum and dad. I remember it being the next day because I'd planned to be cool and not tell Irf about the runs, and blurting it out as soon as he got in the car.

This was the last time we would go anywhere as a family. It was one of those 'last shot' trips. Me and Irf did our best to keep out of it. We'd loaded up with a few taped-up tennis balls and an old yet beautifully weighted Warsop Stebbing.

Outside this sad, rented cottage we played and we played. I concentrated on developing my Nasser backlift: the stiffly cocked wrist, the angled pick-up out to gully, the exaggerated crouch and the floating front foot with toes pointing up. While Irf just ran in hard all day, as he would, as he did.

Phil Walker is editor-in-chief of *Wisden Cricket Monthly* and formerly editor of *All Out Cricket* magazine.

Mike Atherton falls one short of his hundred at Lord's

SAM PERRY

1993/94

AUSTRALIA'S GAME CATCHES FIRE

Warne, the Waughs and a decade of dominance

I can see the sky now. A flaming red enveloped the entire panorama. Embers flitted and twirled balletically into our suburban backyard; slowly at first, then building. Dad told us the way to detect if the bushfires were close was to feel the embers for heat. If they were cool, then so were we. If they were hot, it was time to worry.

It was Sydney in January, 1994. Bushfires raged around the state; some of the worst on record. I was a kid, and didn't really understand the magnitude of it all.

I reflect with a little guilt that the falling embers – which thankfully didn't result in fire reaching my family's house – were a mere annoyance for me. Embers meant we had to stay inside. Ergo, no backyard cricket with my dad, or my uncles, or next-door neighbours, or George from the corner store who just wanted to get back to the shop.

The metaphor is probably crass, but the 1993/94 season was when cricket lit me up. And how could it not? Not only did both sides of my family love the game, but I'm also part of that monumentally blessed cohort whose birthday left me perfectly primed to ride the wave of Australian cricketing supremacy – their hegemony only ending for me at age 20 in September 2005 as I promoted premium beer to wealthy punters late at night:

Imprinting is rapid learning that occurs during a brief receptive period, and establishes a long-lasting behavioural response to a specific individual or object, as attachment to parent, offspring, or site.

And so, in imprinting terms, I was a duckling and Shane Warne was my mother. Imagine if one of your earliest memories of international cricket was 'The Gatting Ball'. Recovery from addiction would be impossible, and so it's proved. But if that ball in the Australian winter of 1993 was

Dean Jones revolutionised the art of one-day batting

Warne's greatest-ever hit, his performance against South Africa later that summer was his early-years magnum opus. I watched, mouth agape, as the blond bombshell, pre-shoulder and pre-finger injury, enacted the fullest expression of his freakish abilities.

We'd only just begun to understand Warne at that point. It wasn't just his array of deliveries, it was the way they were received by batsmen. He regularly confounded and bemused them; a young Copperfield dazzling children on a street corner, except these were seasoned international batsmen.

Listen to Richie Benaud's commentary early in Warne's first spell against South Africa at Sydney. Daryll Cullinan punishes Warne's flipper to the boundary. Then a half-tracker gets dispatched through point for another four. "Well, that looked to me to be the one Warne shows them," he said. And he was right. Warne nailed Cullinan with a flipper shortly thereafter, having set him up with loose deliveries.

Imagine being so good as to countenance bowling *deliberately* loose deliveries at Test level, not yet 10 Tests into your career. Warne went on to take 12-128 in the match, a figure emblazoned into my memory after a *Sunday Herald* tribute became poster material, stuck gleefully onto my bedroom wall.

Just next to my bedroom was a little front room, where an itchy, generations-old couch faced an equally dated TV – one of those that required the twisting of a dial to change the channel. If this reeks of a 'simpler times' vibe, that's because it was. In between sessions of *Alex Kidd* on Sega Master System II, my elder sister and I would watch the music chart countdown on ABC's *Rage*, where I co-opted her passion for seeing Bryan Adams' *Please Forgive Me* surge up the charts. I can vividly recall the tenderness of that film clip: we savoured it each week, as that was the only time we'd be able to see it. I still think it's a decent tune.

I remember hearing my parents talking about PM Paul Keating, whose signature policy was the passing of the Native Title Act, which defended land rights for our indigenous brothers and sisters. They listened to Crowded House, INXS, Cold Chisel, Midnight Oil. And cricket was on all the time. Not just the international caper, but state stuff too. These were the Mercantile Mutual Cup fixtures, where the interest was such that North Sydney Oval would be close to packed, and we'd urge New South Wales players like Wayne Holdsworth, Brad McNamara, Richard Chee Quee and Shane Lee over the line. These guys were cult heroes then; I'd struggle to name any state player who'd fit into that category now.

I cannot mention this summer without referencing the Benson & Hedges World Series. It disappoints the purist in me to write this, but day-night cricket in coloured clothing captivated me at age nine far more than Test cricket did. It's probably why the T20 marketeers have it right. I still remember haranguing my parents for an Australian one-day shirt, the one in the famous lightning fashion. They suggested I opt for the more classic shoulder-stripe arrangement adorned by NSW. I was persuaded, and even though

I was able to get so much mileage out of that shirt (I once went as 'Mark Waugh 1993/94' to a fancy dress 21st), I still regret the choice to this day. For a 33-year-old, I think about it far too much.

But I now recognise I was lucky. My parents' love for the game, and the fact that they could afford some nice things, meant I had exposure to the SCG members at this time too. Unlike other grounds around Australia, the players sit in very close proximity to other members, with the home dressing room sufficiently lowered so as to allow kids the chance to wave miniature bats in the eyeline of players, like seagulls bellowing for signatures.

There were different rules for different players. The Waugh brothers rarely gave signatures at the game. When they did, it was a reward for manners. They were very big on manners. The bowlers were great: I must have got Paul Reiffel's signature eight times, same with Tim May and early-years Glenn McGrath.

But it was one otherwise-nondescript fixture where my signature hunting reached its peak. I was milling around with other kids outside the dressing room at the dinner break in a day-nighter between Australia and New Zealand, waiting to see if anyone would come out to sign.

I wasn't a front-pack hunter; I would never beckon players out. I would wait, shyly, at the back, and queue patiently if a player decided to practise his penmanship. Dean Jones – my favourite player – then came out onto the balcony. He surveyed the scene: dozens of kids squawking, miniature bats and club cricket caps raised in one hand, Staedtler pens or Sharpies in the other. I just stood at the back, watching. We caught eyes briefly, or so I thought. He then walked back into the changing room and emerged with a pair of gloves. He looked at me, underarm-lobbed them over the hunting pack, and straight into my hands. I can still see him now, zinc lashed across the bottom lip, mouthing the words, "They're yours".

There was a commotion. I ran like the wind back to the seat next to Dad, more elated than I'd ever been in life up to that point. The gloves were new. They smelt great. A small green square on the back of them had a gold Kookaburra emblazoned on it. They were signed.

Jones was batting in his customary position at No.3 in that match. I was genuinely worried he'd go out to face Pringle, Cairns, Larsen and co. without gloves. He was okay. He made 21 off 41 balls. Australia lost by 13 runs.

Years later, I'd wear those gloves in my first season of cricket. They stretched up to my elbows, but I didn't care. They were an ornament to my favourite summer of cricket, which had given me Warne, the Mercantile Mutual Cup and Dean Jones and his gloves.

Weeks after the event, that love – so fast and so strong – would compel me to pick up hot, bushfire-induced embers, and think, 'Can we still play cricket?'.

Sam Perry is a writer-journalist and the host and founder of *The Grade Cricketer* podcast.

EMMA JOHN

1994

BAD THINGS HAPPEN TO GOOD PEOPLE

A new era for English cricket under a bright young captain would turn, predictably enough, into a feeding frenzy

I spent a lot of time reading dystopian novels in my early teenage years. My friends and I may have been too early for *The Hunger Games*, but we shared well-thumbed copies of *1984* and *The Handmaid's Tale*, and endless stories set in the aftermath of nuclear holocaust. These kind of terrifyingly bleak reads were, in many ways, a good grounding for the apocalyptic world of England cricket of the 1990s – an age when bad things happened to good people, and every child's dream was crushed by the totalitarian horror of a savage and ruthless Australian machine.

But it wasn't always like that.

There was hope, once; the promise of a different future. In 1994 – before the invincible empire of Steve Waugh began to rise, and his enforcer, Darth Warne, held our throats in his

death grip – Mike Atherton's team were about to play New Zealand on their own (damp, seaming) turf. New players were being blooded under a young captain and there was still the potential for any one of them – Craig White, perhaps, or Steve Rhodes – to emerge as a Jedi.

England had lost to the West Indies in the winter of 1993/94, but they'd shown some guts against the formidable attack of Courtney Walsh and Curtly Ambrose. Now they faced a Test side that had, in their history of 65 Test series, won just four. The series was a kind of teething ring; something to chew on, to develop some bite, before England sat down at the grown-ups' table with South Africa later in the summer.

It was also something of a training toy for me: the first home series I'd approached as a fully-fledged fan. I'd fallen for the game midway through the Ashes series the previous year, and spent the winter swotting up, learning everything I could about cricket from books, from newspapers, and from my mother. I was still woefully naïve, of course. I believed in the England team as I had never believed in anything before – not Christmas, not my Brownie Guide promise, not even the fact that my dad knew everything.

But this was a heady time. As a teenager, I demonstrated the classic adolescent duality of enervating hopelessness and aggressive self-righteousness. (No doubt this was why I enjoyed the dystopian fiction so much.) The world was – without doubt – a terrible and futile place, being destroyed by venal, self-important old men. Only clear-sighted, pure-hearted youth could save it from its doomed trajectory. Atherton's new England were part of that campaign.

The Kiwi team were also favouring youth over experience. In Shane Thomson, Stephen Fleming and the 22-year-old Dion Nash they even had a few players whose pictures wouldn't disgrace a schoolgirl's locker wall. (Not mine, I hasten to add. I was far too loyal for that.) The series was a demonstration of potential rather than proficiency, and when England won the ODI series and the first Test – by an innings – it confirmed my conviction that I had joined this sport at the dawning of a new era.

It didn't dampen my celebrations in the least that the ODI victory had consisted of a single game (the other was rained off), or that England only saved the second Test by the skin of Steve Rhodes' bat, when the wicketkeeper blocked out the final session with a dwindling tail for company. They couldn't finish the Kiwi batsmen off in the third Test at Old Trafford either. But how was a novice like me to know that a 1-0 victory over Ken Rutherford and a largely crocked Mark Greatbatch was not something you should get excited about?

I learned fast, that summer. When Kepler Wessels' South Africa arrived, their rainbow flag resplendent on the visitors' balcony at Lord's, I realised for the first time that cricket was about far more than what happened on the field of play. And if the celebration of South Africa's return from sporting purdah engendered high emotion – well, so did the discovery that Atherton had been walking around with pockets full of dirt, which he'd been nonchalantly applying to the ball.

My chief impression of the furore that followed – the fines, the press conferences, one newspaper's demand to "show us your trousers" – was that being England cricket captain is a more highly scrutinised position than the Archbishop of Canterbury. And that anyone squeamish at the sight of a man being hounded to resign his job won't last long a sports fan. If I'd been baptised into the faith of England cricket in 1993, then Pocketgate was my confirmation, my coming of age, and the moment I realised that martyrdom was an inbuilt part of the cause.

Still, looking back at a distance of 20 years, it's not the hard lessons that prevail. Whatever worldliness I acquired that summer, it's the scent of hopefulness that still wafts down the decades. The way Darren Gough bounded into my consciousness for the first time, against New Zealand at Old Trafford, England 235-7, a stocky 23-year-old with gelled hair and limpid blue eyes strutting to the crease, and blasting a half-century with an abandon I had not before seen in an England batsman, much less a No.9. The way his skiddy bowling hurried and hustled the granite-faced South Africans. The way his joyous grin reflected in the fielders' faces around him.

If there was a pinnacle to that summer's optimism, it was Devon Malcolm's bowling at The Oval, a climactic end to a tumultuous season. I remember a few of the deliveries – the one that sent Jonty Rhodes to hospital, for instance. But I also remember the contributions others made, be it Joey Benjamin's four wickets in the first innings, or Rhodes leaping, salmon-like, to take a catch off Craig Matthews. Most of all I remember Phillip DeFreitas running full pelt to snaffle a boundary catch on his knees, then jumping up straight to applaud the bowler. It was an image of a team invested in each other.

We thought, then, that Malcolm's devastating nine-fer was a teaser trailer for more blockbusting feats to come. In fact, it was the peak of his powers, a perfect and cosmically rare alignment of pace and accuracy. It stood throughout the decade that followed as an embodiment of promise unfulfilled – just one more flash of St Elmo's Fire, dazzling us with its electric light, signifying nothing. But oh, how beautiful it was.

Emma John is an author and journalist whose first book, *Following On: A Memoir of Teenage Obsession and Terrible Cricket,* was named the 2017 Wisden Book of the Year.

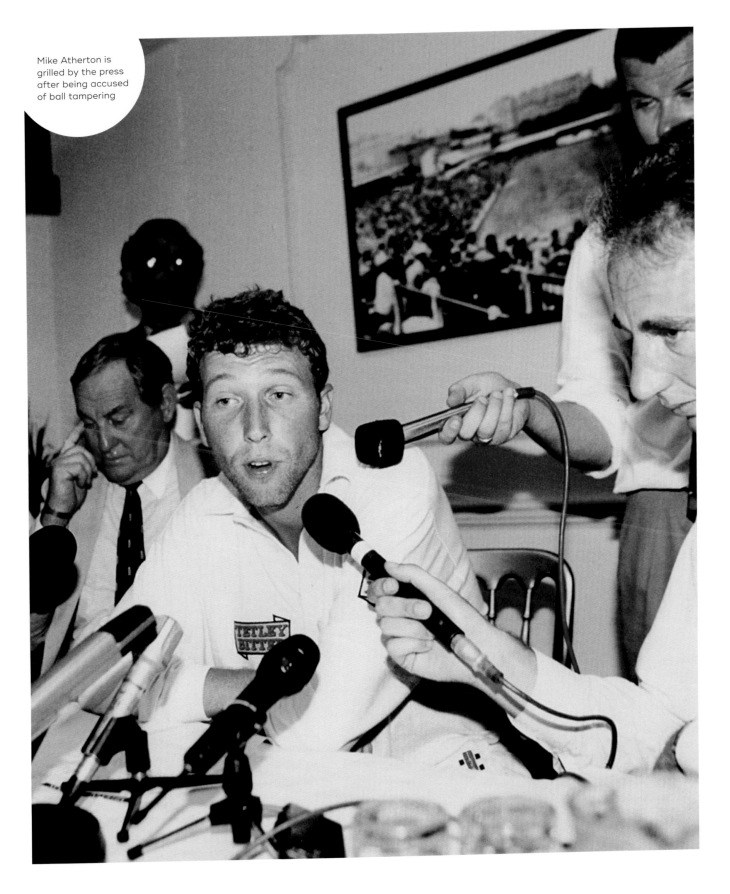

Mike Atherton is grilled by the press after being accused of ball tampering

Michael Bevan
starred for Australia's
second string in the
Benson & Hedges
World Series

ADAM COLLINS

1994/95

AUSTRALIA CALLS IN
THE A-TEAM

*While the 1994/95 Ashes series was largely one-way traffic, it was the
formation of Australia's 'A' team that really captured the imagination*

When I think back to the best days of
my childhood, the image is always one
blessed Australian summer, a catalogue
of moments and scores that remain
instantly recognisable. More than two
decades on, its months still feel endless.

As a lad of 10 years, I was just old
enough to be transfixed by every vagary of our game, and
to play competitively. It may have erred on the side of
monocultural, but the country of my upbringing was also
vastly simpler. The only Waughs to be concerned with were
in the middle order, not the Middle East. Parochialism felt
natural and inclusive, rather than confused nationalism or
worse. And we knew it mattered when the English came to
town as they did in 1994/95. So we roared when Michael
Slater slayed the Poms at Brisbane and laughed with joy when

Shane Warne skittled Alec Stewart with his best flipper yet.
Ominous beginnings.

Christmas brought my own debut, of sorts: heading to
the mighty MCG to watch Test cricket in the flesh. It was a
novelty that would become a ritual, then an obsession, and
eventually a career.

On this day, from the back of the Southern Stand, I saw David
Boon carefully compile his 20th Test ton, leaving no doubt of
his standing. But it was one ball from Damien Fleming that
fuelled me; an unplayable outswinger to Graeme Hick that
crashed into off stump. My joy at witnessing this particular part
of the bowling craft has never abated. Warne's hat-trick the next
morning was euphoric; our own, unstoppable hometown genius,
back before he singlehandedly kept the tabloids in business.

Sydney's New Year Test represented the middle of the series,
not the hurried end to a tour it has since become. It was

there that a young bloke called Darren Gough ran through Australia like no Englishman had in a generation, and he sure was easy to like for his eager celebrations after each wicket and occasional change-up leg-break.

In Adelaide, on Australia Day weekend, Greg Blewett's debut century felt more significant than England's sole victory, coming as it did so long after they had arrived. By now, their misadventure was comical; illustrated by the fact that even the team physio had to cut short his tour after injuring himself during a stint as a substitute fielder.

Order was restored in Perth, in a match notable for Slater's third audacious ton of the series, England's many dropped catches and a last goodbye for Graham Gooch and Mike Gatting. Graham Thorpe's own excellent century was the only positive the visitors could take. It was an appropriate finale to an altogether shambolic three months for England, while Australia were primed to leap to the top of the world in the Caribbean three months later.

For all the Ashes mystique, the white-ball fare – meshed between Tests in an era where squads seldom changed between formats – elicits memories just as vivid. While the annual limited-overs tournament was a staple, this time it had a twist. The gap in standard between England and their hosts – and the newly arrived Zimbabwe squad – presented fears of a gravely uncompetitive tri-series. So administrators found a solution: expanding the tournament to four teams, including an Australia 'A' side. It was a revelation.

The young understudies became the nation's sweethearts in the best tradition of the underdog. Forget Taylor, Slater, Waugh, Warne, McGrath and company – we wanted a top order of Blewett, Hayden, Ponting, Martyn, Bevan, Langer and Lehmann. One after another, they would announce themselves. And it worked: fast-forward eight years, to the Ashes series of 2002/03, and five of Australia's top six emerged during that summer.

Australian flags were brought to games with giant 'A's painted on them to show their support, even when competing with the senior side. Indeed, captain Mark Taylor's annoyance was palpable when the Adelaide crowd barracked against the 'real' Australia in favour of the kids. On this basis, it was explained, the innovation wouldn't continue for more than a season.

The brilliant theatre came to a climax when the 'A' team defeated England in their last group game – prompting a headline that England wouldn't beat Australia 'Z' – to secure a spot in the best-of-three finals against the top dogs. Bevan's run-a-ball century was a sign of things to come.

In the lead-up to the deciders, Paul Reiffel – who had led the 'A' team's attack throughout – was given a promotion, but, curiously, only to carry drinks for Taylor's men. At home we fumed, spouting conspiracy theories. These games may not have carried formal ODI status, but that meant nothing by now; they were our guys. One banner quipped, with a nod to the sponsor Toyota: 'Australia plays with itself, oh what a feeling!'

In place of Reiffel, Greg Rowell – who later tried his hand at politics – bowled the final over at the SCG with three runs to defend. The crowd roared for him to keep Steve Waugh at bay, especially after a couple of dot balls. Rowell stared down the Australian hard man. It was the best cricket all summer. The 'A's didn't win, but by then it didn't matter.

Many years later, upon seeing a man in a pub wearing one of the predominantly green 'A' playing shirts from that summer, I very seriously offered him what amounted to about half my week's wages to buy it. He refused my offer; there was just no way he would part with that. They were his guys too.

To Victorian eyes, the raw deal handed to the 'A's was just the latest slight to add to our existing outrage. We were already occupied with another injustice; the ongoing exclusion of Dean Jones from national squads of both varieties, even after a triple century in a Sheffield Shield game played under lights with a yellow ball, the precursor to the pink. He led the state to a win in the domestic one-day competition, in uniforms that did away with traditional trousers in favour of jaunty blue shorts. How didn't that catch on? Of course, Queensland did win the Shield for the first time that season, but no summer is truly perfect.

All the while in the suburban under-12 third-division comp, I charged in just as hard as I did in the driveway with my brother and mates, on arenas where bad light didn't exist; hurling the ball down at each other well beyond dusk, tattered baseball caps held together by tape. The quintessential story of Australian summer is mine as much as anyone's.

Is the retention of information about cricket of long ago a blessing, or just clogging up bandwidth that could be more meaningfully deployed? Probably a bit of both. But it means my one crowded summer is never far away.

Adam Collins is an Australian writer and broadcaster. He co-hosts *The Final Word* podcast and is *Wisden Cricket Monthly*'s Australia correspondent.

ROSS
ARMSTRONG

1995

THEATRES OF
DREAMS

*A cussed masterpiece encapsulates the full gamut
of human experience*

s my tired hippocampus ticks on past another year of service, the early Nineties seem to have bled together into one smooth summer of airplane trails across blue skies, endless smartphone-free hours of staring at things, and long, hot journeys in the back of my dad's car, as I accompanied him and my mum on exotic work trips to places that either looked like Maidstone, or were Maidstone.

What I certainly remember is cricket, teletext, and watching England play cricket for hours, mostly on teletext – 302 for football, 340 for cricket. I still remember the numbers you had to punch in on hotel room televisions if you wanted to avoid lines of data that described holidays you should never go on, but we sometimes did.

I also remember asking for a guitar and my mother immediately going out and buying me a clarinet. Hoping my grandad would live longer, but instead getting a Sega Mega Drive. And asking to see Manchester United, but being taken to see Worcestershire at New Road. It's still the greatest enforced compromise I've ever made, my dad's finest hour and one of the best days of my life.

I remember the immediate inclusivity of the low hum of old fellas muttering about 'actions' on wooden benches in a strange pastoral paradise. A man called Richard Illingworth with the air of a village minister returning to his fielding position, being applauded for his very existence, and doffing his cap in thanks for the recognition. The bafflement of trying to get used to the pace with which the ball went from hand to bat, then sometimes to boundary, which didn't happen as much in the Sunday League as it does now but that just made it better when it did. In fact, scratch that; a huge bloke called Tom Moody was opening up for us and I think he broke the club shop window, but as I've been unable to verify this it may be my mind telling lies. But he did get a tantalising 99 not out as Worcestershire won by 10 wickets.

I went out on the pitch and got Stuart Lampitt's autograph, and an unattractive pear-coloured jumper that I would intermittently wear for at least 10 fashion-baiting years, often claiming irony if asked, but really in remembrance of that day.

But I don't want to talk about that. Not in the main. I want to talk about the English cricket team in 1995. The year began as time itself surely did: with England already two Tests down in Australia. Worcestershire's Steve Rhodes was keeping wicket for England, which made sense to me, Graeme Hick was batting at three, which made more, but big Tom Moody wasn't playing for Australia, which made even less sense than the lack of girls flocking to me after my clarinet recitals in assembly.

The list of English bowlers made interesting reading too. Being largely a teletext watcher, I'd judge players first and foremost on the strength of their names: as I couldn't pronounce Shaun Udal, I decided he couldn't be that good. I loved Devon Malcolm, as every normal man-human should, having seen his ferocious run-up on TV. The name McCague didn't sound good to me, and Benjamin seemed like the sort of boy at school that would be 'too into books', so I didn't predict great things from them. Before you criticise my methods, history seems to have proved me correct. History also had varying fortunes ahead for Tufnell and Lewis, although if you'd asked me I'd have said they were both thoroughly reliable characters in name and action. And I knew enough to trust Fraser, Gough and DeFreitas from what I'd seen; thoroughly reliable sorts who bounded in with their ample arses.

The third Test, the first game for 'England 1995', proved them much better than that 'England 1994' side; Darren Gough taking the Man of the Match award and the Aussies hanging on for a draw in dying light. They were even better in the next Test, Phil DeFreitas' 88 from the lower order leading England to victory. Just by way of colour we lost the final Test by 329 runs, but as dead rubbers don't count I called that a 1-0 victory for 'England 1995'.

Next up was the tantalising prospect of a summer visit by the West Indies. DeFreitas was dropped for the first Test in favour of the solidly named Peter Martin, who, while he had his moments, wasn't to become the England legend that his stalwart name suggested he should. We lost.

The second Test belonged to a debutant who was to become one of two new heroes for me that year: Dominic Cork, who took a seven-fer, which won the match and a small part of my cricket heart. England, however, were thrashed in the third Test, and when I left with the 'rents for a holiday in France, things were not looking up for 'England 1995'. And yet, by the time we returned, the green isle was bathed in sunshine and a friend of my dad's quickly ushered me into his living room to show me Cork's hat-trick, which he'd recorded on VHS. For the first, but certainly not the last time, the cricket and the weather combined to give me the feeling that everything in the world was peaceful and beautiful and right.

The series ended a thoroughly entertaining 2-2 draw and it seemed like the next day that England jetted off to play South Africa. The village minister-a-like Illingworth was in the side by then, which made utter sense to me, and I followed every warm-up match, analysing his figures each night so I could picture how he was bowling. But the second hero of 1995 comes rather late to this story. At times, this five-Test series, that somehow included four draws, seemed to me like the most important thing that had ever happened anywhere, ever. And most of these times involved Allan Donald, in fearsome form, and that hero and bastion of utter English cricketness, Michael Atherton.

Every He-Man needs his Skeletor, every Hulk Hogan needs his Undertaker, every boy needs his clarinet; because it's the brilliance of the adversary that makes heroes what they are. On December 4, 1995, during Atherton's 10-and-a-half hour marathon innings of 185 not out, he stood firm against bowling that was dangerous to his stumps and all the best bones in his body. Atherton's innings didn't just *have* everything, it *was* everything: it was politics, it was a wrestling match, it was scones and jam under a broken umbrella in the rain, it was the definition of stoicism in all languages, it was winning a Droitwich Spa pub quiz, it was the opening scene of *Saving Private Ryan*, it was going fast down that hill at the end of our road when the sun was out, it was copying all your Nirvana albums to minidisc, it was two men blessed respectively with skill and will, watched by a small percentage of the world, as if the fate of humanity depended on it.

And the result was a draw. And I knew for sure that my heart was lost forever.

Ross Armstrong is a writer and actor who has published two novels, and was the co-creator of the cult podcast, *The Cricket Podblast*.

Richard Illingworth, the former England and Worcestershire left–arm spinner

JO HARMAN

1997

NEW HOPE, NEW LABOUR AND BEN HOLLIOAKE

The summer of 1997 witnessed the emergence of an all-rounder as exciting as English cricket had seen in a generation

My childhood memories generally revolve around either playing or watching sport. Not much of the other stuff really stuck. One non-sport-related memory that has stayed with me, though, is watching the 1992 UK General Election results from my grandparents' bungalow in Hamilton, New Zealand, and seeing the expression on my parents' faces as a tearful red-headed man without much hair gave his resignation speech. Apparently he'd told everyone he was going to win. A lot of people had believed him.

I was seven at the time and didn't understand what it all meant but I did know it was important. That much was clear from my parents' reaction. So when the summer of 1997 began with a landslide win for New Labour, even as a pre-teen with only the most basic grasp of politics I felt the ripples from the wave of optimism that was sweeping the country. Eighteen years of Tory rule were over, and things could only get better with Tony in charge.

And things really did get better, almost instantly. At least in the world of a sport-obsessed 12-year-old. Three weeks later David Hopkin sent Crystal Palace back into the Premier League with a curled last-minute winner at Wembley. I celebrated Palace's return to the top tier by using my birthday money to buy a whole heap of crap from the club shop – bed sheets, towel, lamp, Stevie Coppell figurine – to go alongside my posters of Dean Gordon and Neil Shipperley.

The day before the play-off final I'd been up to London with Dad for the third ODI against Australia at Lord's. Weirdly, England had already won the series – Mike Atherton's century at The Oval two days earlier giving the hosts an unassailable 2-0 lead – and it gave them the chance to experiment by

Ben Hollioake made a
37-ball half-century
on his ODI debut

handing a debut to Surrey's 19-year-old all-rounder Ben Hollioake. Dad and I took a trip to watch England at Lord's each year and tradition dictated that we would leave Canterbury at the crack of dawn, a picnic hamper packed safely in the boot, to watch the players net before play started. On that morning I remember an England fan shouting out to Hollioake in the nets: "Ben, where are you batting?" "Three," he replied. These days he'd probably be reprimanded by the ICC Anti-Corruption Unit for sharing information potentially worth thousands of pounds.

I seem to remember Dad being a bit sceptical that Hollioake would actually bat that high. He'd batted as low as No.8 for Surrey that season and it was generally assumed that he'd been picked more for his seamers. It was also most un-English,

particularly at that time, to throw a debutant teenager, in his first full season of county cricket, in at first drop against the Aussies. Even his older brother wasn't sure he was ready.

"David Graveney [England's chairman of selectors] rang me and said, 'We're going to pick your brother, do you think he's ready?" recalls Adam Hollioake, Ben's captain at Surrey who was also in the team for the Lord's ODI. "I said, 'Well, no I don't, but with him you never know', because that's the way he was. I knew he was going to be good enough but at that stage I didn't think he had much behind him, to recover if things went wrong."

Atherton had evidently seen something special in Ben and England's captain asked him on the morning of the match – presumably only minutes before Dad and I watched him in the

Ben and Adam Hollioake were the only brothers to make their Test debuts together in the 20th century

nets – whether he fancied going in at No.3 as a pinch-hitter. "He shrugged and said, in his laconic way, he'd give it a go," said Atherton.

Six overs into England's reply to Australia's 269 and Hollioake passed his skipper as he walked to the middle – Atherton dismissed by Michael Kasprowicz for a 22-minute innings which comprised a single run – and so began one of the more extraordinary debut innings English cricket has witnessed. There's a short film of the knock on YouTube that you have to watch. Third ball Holloake plays a perfectly timed straight drive which is past Glenn McGrath before he can even react. From there he just keeps going, completely uninhibited by the occasion or the opposition.

The swept six off Shane Warne is the innings' headline shot but my personal favourite is a wonderfully languid lofted straight drive that leaves McGrath chuntering as he collects his sweater from the umpire. You can imagine McGrath thinking, 'Who the hell does this kid think he is?'. And who *did* he think he was? An upstart kid without a record to speak of, flaying the Aussies around HQ as though he didn't have a care in the world. It was so untempered, naïve almost, and when he slapped Jason Gillespie straight to point – falling for a 48-ball 63, 50 of those runs scored in boundaries – it didn't really matter. In just over an hour at the crease he'd played an innings that would never be forgotten by anyone who saw it.

"I was gobsmacked," says his brother Adam. "In awe of how unfazed he was by the situation. He was batting as if it was me and him having a game in the backyard, it just so happened to be against two of the best bowlers of all-time. I knew he could play but I'd be lying if I said I thought a 19-year-old could ever do that to Warne and McGrath. As for Ben, I don't think anything took him by surprise. I put watching that innings up there with my favourite moments from my career."

Seven weeks later, Dad and I were back at Lord's. Kent had reached the Benson & Hedges Cup final where they would be taking on Surrey, and I was in a dilemma. I'd grown up obsessing about Kent – writing out my predicted XIs ahead of the next Sunday's big AXA Equity & Law League clash at St Lawrence, hunting out players' autographs – and I was as desperate for them to lift the trophy as I had been for Palace to win the play-off final earlier that summer. But batting at No.3 for Surrey would be my new hero. As I sat in the car on the drive up to London I was hoping for a Kent win and a Ben Holloake century.

In the end I didn't get either, but we were treated to another Holloake masterclass. Kent's 212 was never going

to be enough against a batting line-up that featured Stewart, Brown, Butcher, Thorpe and the Holloakes, and Surrey cruised to their target with five overs and eight wickets to spare. Holloake was named Player of the Match at Lord's for the second time that summer, playing beautifully once again against a strong attack which included Headley, McCague, Ealham and the Zimbabwean leggie Paul Strang. Holloake eventually fell to Strang two short of a maiden professional hundred. It would prove to be his career-best one-day score. Adam Holloake dedicated the victory to Graham Kersey, Surrey's young wicketkeeper who had died tragically earlier that year in a car crash in Australia.

A month after Surrey's B&H Cup win, the Holloakes made their Test debuts alongside each other in the fifth Ashes Test at Trent Bridge. England were 2-1 down in the series with two to play and Ben and Adam were brought in to add fresh impetus to a side that had gone flat since winning the first Test at Edgbaston. Ben was England's youngest Test player since Brian Close in 1949. He made a classy first-innings 28 but proved expensive with the ball in a heavy defeat and was dropped for the consolation win at The Oval. He finished the summer on a high, though, being named the Cricket Writers' Club Young Cricketer of the Year and receiving the same accolade from the Professional Cricketers' Association.

Kent would end the season as nearly men, finishing runners-up in the Championship (by four points), Sunday League (by two points), as well as losing that B&H Cup final. But what remains most vivid from that summer are those two innings from a player described by Alec Stewart as "the most naturally gifted cricketer that I have ever played alongside".

When five years later, on March 23, 2002, I woke up to the news that Holloake had been killed in a car crash after his Porsche 294 came off a ramp on a Perth expressway and hit a wall, I felt even more privileged to have witnessed his golden summer first hand. Aged 24 and 132 days, no England Test cricketer had died so young.

The four seasons that followed his breakthrough had been a struggle for Holloake, with just one further Test cap, a handful of ODIs and a modest county record. But, having seen what I did at Lord's that summer, there was no doubt in my mind that Holloake was going to be a star.

Jo Harman is magazine editor of *Wisden Cricket Monthly*. He edited *Cricketing Allsorts: The good, the bad, the ugly (and the downright weird)*, published by Wisden in 2017.

JOHN STERN

1997/98

YOUTH AND
YOUNG MANHOOD

*Under African skies, England's likely lads turned up the formbook at the
Under-19 World Cup*

I sat next to an 18-year-old Rob Key on the plane. Just as we were getting ready for take-off, he turned and asked: "Who are you? Not another fitness trainer?" The joke was on both of us, frankly.

Key was a member of the 16-strong England under 19s squad setting off for a tour of South Africa that would culminate in a youth World Cup tournament, whose one and only previous edition had been in 1988. I was a young journalist, at 27, roughly a decade older than the players but, like them, hoping to further my career with a few eye-catching performances on tour.

I'd just gone freelance after five years at the renowned Hayters agency. Having spent my days trying vainly to tease exclusives from the likes of Harry Redknapp and Mick McCarthy, it was time to go all in with my first love, cricket.

The senior England team were often hapless and in the summer of 1997 they'd taken another Ashes beating. The likes of *The Times* and the *Telegraph* were keen to cover the exploits of the next generation. This was also a chance to get to know the future stars of English cricket, and visit a spectacular country.

The players and I weren't the only ones on a mission. The members of the small support staff were also on a journey of sorts. Phil Neale was the manager, honing his administrative credentials for grander challenges ahead. He's just retired as operations manager of the England men's side after the best part of 20 years. For the coach, John Abrahams, a trip to South Africa had a deeper significance. His father Cec was a peer of Basil D'Oliveira's and, like Dolly, was a highly talented cricketer, condemned to playing on the margins of this segregated society. He came to England where he settled in the north-west and was a stalwart of the Lancashire leagues. His son would go on to captain Lancashire.

Owais Shah lifts
the Under 19 World
Cup trophy

The Rainbow Nation was in its infancy. It had been only three years since the first multi-racial general election in South Africa. Naively I expected to be hit by the sweet smell of newly embraced liberalism and open-mindedness. Not so much. One early conversation with a (white) umpire stays with me. He was talking about his love of English football. I expressed excitement on his behalf that South Africa would be participating in their first World Cup in France the following year. He wasn't fussed. He supported England, he said, and in any case South Africa were rubbish. OK, but still your country's qualified for the World Cup, that's pretty cool. He wasn't having any of it and only at this point did it start to dawn on me what might be underpinning his position. But I wanted to hear it. So I asked him directly why. "Well, it's a black team," he said casually. The only thing more offensive than his flagrant racism was that he seemed to presume that I, as a white man, would share – or at least understand – his toxic opinion.

Both Neale and Abrahams – and the engagingly eccentric physio, Stuart Robertson, from Sussex – were exceptionally welcoming. Among my reporting tasks was supplying content for the ECB's embryonic website so I was, in effect, embedded with the team. I travelled and socialised with the squad. It was a privileged position that tested boundaries of trust on both sides. It also challenged my deadlines – with a number of clients to service immediately after the close of play, it was a rush to get all my work done and still make it on to the team bus.

Mostly this worked out fine. On one occasion though, at Newlands in Cape Town, I walked round to the back of the pavilion from the press box to see a disconcerting absence of transport. This was a problem because the team were moving on to Paarl, an hour's drive away, for the next match. I phoned Abrahams. "Oh shit, we've left Sterny behind," he blurted out, presumably to his colleague, Neale. I decided to check myself into the adjacent Holiday Inn and worry about getting to Paarl in the morning. Instead, though, the team's South African liaison officer drove from Paarl to Newlands to pick me up. It was, as the great West Country writer David Foot would say, 'a splendid gesture'.

There were chaotic elements to the tour. Match venues changed for not entirely clear reasons. Accommodation did too, mostly at the request of Neale, who had to make the most of his contacts with the likes of Ali Bacher to keep the show on the road. The England players might have been full-time pro cricketers but the South Africans tended to view them more like a schoolboy side.

There was plenty of talent in the squad. Captained by Owais Shah, it contained a smattering of future internationals. Graeme Swann and Paul Franks were the ones who showed true mettle in the first part of the trip but there was a lot of attitude and not much application. It took a four-hour innings of 32 not out from Michael Gough (aka 'the Bradman of umpiring') to save the first of the two four-day 'Tests' against South Africa under 19s.

Life on tour was fun. The sun was hot and the beer was cheap, though I worried that getting too close to the players would compromise any notion I had of editorial independence. Most didn't know – or maybe didn't care – what I was writing, though I recall one exchange with Ian Flanagan, an opening batsman from Essex. "I heard you got stuck into me in the paper," he said one day. "Really? Who told you that?" "My mum." "Did she tell you what I wrote?" "No." "Well, I think I said that you played round a straight one." "Fair enough." It was a reminder to be fair and factual in one's criticism even if the recipient's response to it might be neither of those things.

Christmas was bizarre. We arrived in Johannesburg on Christmas Eve in the pouring rain, spent the next day at Sun City and Boxing Day eating a very moderate Xmas dinner and playing out a version of *Blind Date*, scripted by Abrahams in which I played the part of the aforementioned Key. It was a good distraction for a bunch of teenagers – never mind the oldies – who were unused to being away from home for such an extended period.

England won only two of their 11 games leading into the World Cup. By the time it started, we'd been on tour for the best part of seven weeks. It didn't feel like the players were about to peak for the big games. Yet that's exactly what happened. They qualified from their group on net run-rate, though if their defeat by Bangladesh had been more severe they'd have been knocked out.

Pakistan, with Abdul Razzaq, Shoaib Malik and Imran Tahir, were the first opponents in the Super League stage. England won by 18 runs with three of Essex's five squad members to the fore: opener Stephen Peters made 92, Graham Napier took three wickets and Jonathan Powell took a blinding one-handed catch on the boundary. Off-spinner Powell was out of the professional game in two years with a first-class career that comprises three matches, including an England A game.

Defeat to India left England all but out of the tournament. They had to thrash unbeaten Australia, who had Marcus North and Michael Klinger in their ranks. There were about 2,000 people at Newlands to see the swing bowling of Franks and Northants' Richard Logan bundle out the Aussies for 147. Neale had done his homework to know that if England could get the runs inside 30 overs they would get to the final. Incredible to think this information wasn't universally available but that's how it was. England got off to a flyer and Franks secured the match award with a freewheeling 41 off 34 balls. By the time Australia, and their coach Allan Border, realised what was going on it was too late. From the other side of the ground, it was possible to make out plastic chairs going airborne in the Aussie dressing room.

Both teams celebrated/commiserated together in the Green Man pub that night. Border was in a form of fancy dress as punishment for his mathematical oversight – or maybe just for losing to the Poms. England had played two decent games of cricket and they were in a World Cup final.

The night before the game, at a team dinner, I was even asked to address the players, a speech that for some reason I decided to turn into an impression of Alec Stewart. There were at least 5,000 in at the Wanderers for the final against New Zealand, whom England had beaten in their opening match of the tournament. England bowled terribly at the start and the Kiwis were 71-0 from 12 overs. But a bit of canny medium-pace nibble from Napier and Giles Haywood, who played briefly for Sussex and Notts, reined it in. England needed 242 and breezed to victory with four overs to spare. Peters made a stylish century and captain Shah was there at the end 54 not out.

It was a gloriously improbable triumph and gave a group of teenage cricketers their 15 minutes of fame. Some would stay famous, for others it was inevitably fleeting. Some forged high-achieving cricketing careers, others left the professional game almost instantly.

I followed the under 19s side for three more winters but none of those trips came close to this one. The World Cup win was the crowning glory but the friendships and the memories are what last forever.

John Stern is editor-at-large at *Wisden Cricket Monthly* and was formerly editor of *The Wisden Cricketer*. He has written four books on cricket.

Muttiah Muralitharan spins Sri Lanka to victory by taking 16 wickets at The Oval

VITHUSHAN
EHANTHARAJAH

1998

MURALI MAKES SRI LANKAN
VOICES HEARD

*Torn between his Sri Lankan roots and English upbringing, the summer of 1998 provided
our author with a memorable introduction to live Test cricket and a flawed stylist*

I t was only in 1996 that I realised you could boast about being Sri Lankan. Growing up in west London, as a bloody civil war rumbled on in Sri Lanka, my parents had kept the idea of nationality close to their chests. We were Tamil, I knew that much. But Sri Lankan? My parents were not totally keen to commit to that.

My father's family were caught in the crossfire, with various businesses ransacked or burned to the ground. On the eve of my first birthday, my mother lost a sister and brother in mortar attacks. Another brother went missing, only to arrive on our doorstep when I was two or three. My earliest memories are of him cooking and changing me. Only later did I put the pieces together and figure out why he had spent so much time indoors.

With little Sri Lankan influence at home, other than the food we ate and the verbal reprimands I received, I was unequivocally English. In life and sport – England. Until one afternoon in 1996 when we sat in front of a radio to listen to Sri Lanka's World Cup final victory over Australia. My dad gave a wry smile as he rose out of his armchair and, for the first time in my life, he let the veil slip: "I can't believe it – they've won the World Cup!"

Being the only Sri Lankan at school, I received congratulations from other cricket lovers who assumed my house was awash with the yellow, green, orange and maroon. I didn't tell them otherwise. For the first time, there was genuine interest in my background. Interest beyond Mr Brown remarking that I was lucky I'd never have to waste money on sun cream. And he was an arsehole.

I lapped it up. I was both Sri Lankan and English in equal measure. "England for football, Sri Lanka in cricket," I told my classmates, as Euro 96 came and went. "But what happens when England are playing Sri Lanka – who do you support then?" When Sri Lanka arrived for their 1998 tour of England, that bridge needed to be crossed.

By then England had started to stitch some results together and the summer of '98 was the first in which I properly binged on cricket. Aged 12, I was engrossed in what was to be the BBC's last year of live Test cricket.

South Africa were in town and I knew they were good because they had big jaws and Ivan Drago opening the bowling. Having been 1-0 down, England rallied to take the series 2-1, winning the series-decider at Headingley thanks to a century from Mark Butcher, the most bloody-minded 94 from Nasser Hussain and nine and eight wickets in the match for Darren Gough and Angus Fraser respectively. At the end of the broadcast, the coverage threw forward to the final Test of the summer – England were to play a one-off Test against Sri Lanka at The Oval.

Immediately, I asked my dad if we could go. Almost as quickly, the request was rejected. But a few days later he told me that one of his co-workers, who also happened to be a family friend – 'Uncle Raj' – had two spare tickets for day one so my younger brother and me attended what would be our first Test.

I had never even watched Sri Lanka on TV and that mystique alone meant that I would be rooting for them. Mostly I couldn't wait to see Muttiah Muralitharan. It wasn't about the outrageous spin or the shedload of wickets. Here was a Sri Lankan Tamil playing international sport.

We took our seats in the Peter May Stand, surrounded by a few of my dad's work friends. As the day wore on, the air around us went from summer breeze to Stella musk and sweat. The bloke behind us got louder with each English run, at one point proclaiming that he had tits on his head after fashioning a hat out of page three of *The Sun*. Later in the day, as Sri Lanka struggled to get into the game, he asked my brother and me what my dad was doing at short-leg... and slip... and cover... and running in to bowl. I laughed but knew it wasn't funny. My brother, quiet, unassuming – aged seven – emptied half a bag of Bombay Mix into his pint.

On the field, things weren't going as I had hoped. Murali was struggling and, sat side-on, I couldn't really get a grasp of what

it was that made him so great. He'd finish with 16 wickets in a 10-wicket win for Sri Lanka.

At the fall of England's first wicket, out strode Graeme Hick. My immediate thought was, wow, that is *a man*. The game looked unfair for the rest. Hick stood tall at the crease, dwarfed the Sri Lankan fielders and looked far too big in comparison to the stumps. His hundred seemed inevitable. But just as I was developing a new hero, in walked Mark Ramprakash.

Before Ramprakash, I'd viewed batting as just another component of the game. I held bowling in a higher regard as it seemed more box-office. The action starts with a bowler's run-up. To me, the bowler controlled the game. But when Ramprakash came out, the match seemed to bend to his whims. When Hick played a shot, people clapped. When Ramprakash played a shot, they sighed before doing so. He only made 53, but did it with such grace.

Our trip home consisted of me firing questions at Uncle Raj during a pit-stop at McDonald's. "Why didn't Ramprakash get a hundred?" I asked. Uncle Raj laughed: "He does that sometimes." "Do you think he should have got one? I do. Hick got one. Ramprakash should have." Uncle Raj looked at me, I could see the wheels turning. He coached Bessborough in the Middlesex leagues and knew his stuff. I could tell he wanted to break something to me, but seeing I was head over heels he didn't want to tell me that, for his money, after 28 matches and just one century, Ramprakash wasn't cut out for Test cricket, and that he was lucky to keep his place after 249 runs in nine innings against South Africa that summer. That, perhaps, mentally, the highest form of the game asked too much of him.

Instead, he settled for the following: "Batting is too easy for Ramprakash. When you teach someone to bat, you teach them to bat like Ramprakash. Sometimes it doesn't work. Sometimes, you can do everything right but, whether it is God or something else, it does not work out as you want it to. That doesn't mean you stop. Ramprakash will probably score more hundreds for England. But, today, he did everything right and didn't score a hundred. That is cricket."

Vithushan Ehantharajah is a sports features writer for the *Independent*. He previously worked for *Cricbuzz* and was named the Christopher Martin-Jenkins Young Journalist of the Year in 2014 for his coverage of county cricket for *ESPNcricinfo*.

FELIX WHITE

1999

CHASING DOWN EDGES
LIKE IT'S 1999

Even in its final throes, finding meaning in bad cricket remained
the *story of the Nineties*

Ninety-nine was my first Test match. Both mine and Darren Maddy's. At some point in the morning session he manically chased down an outside edge, sliding in on his side semi-convincingly and flinging the ball in to ensure a likely four was kept to three.

Behind me, a couple of men commentating between themselves – interspersing the punditry with tales of who'd left whom and who was after sole custody – took particular note.

"Who was that? Graham Thorpe?"

"No, Darren Maddy. You don't chase anything down like that if you know you're in the side."

To be fair, England's stalwarts did often appear to be inspecting the backs of their fingernails. Still, I couldn't help but feel it was a little unfair. England lost, catastrophically,

and there was something strangely momentous about it. It was tragi-comic. I couldn't necessarily understand what I was feeling, but there was a certain kind of pride to be witnessing it – a kind of learned behaviour, a sense of *theatre* attached to the 'Here we go again' brigade, rolling their eyes across The Oval in collective acceptance of inevitable disappointment. I observed it keenly.

We spent the third session passionately collecting plastic glasses for pint snakes and giggling while frenetically tearing up anything cardboard to throw in the air when the Mexican wave came back around. It was the summer that I started to realise I was probably going to be tied to the endless dimensions of cricket for a very long time.

There was so much about that day that still feels vivid. The personalities of the cricketers themselves, so caricatured and cartoonish even from the back of the Bedser Upper. It was fascinating that Andrew Caddick genuinely cat-walked up to bowl in real life and it wasn't somehow invented through television. Nasser Hussain was all cursing and constant muttering, pumping his chest, walking back towards the crease, taking stance, leaving the ball, repeating the process. He eventually half-hooked a bouncer to square leg, staring through the gas works in the distance, arms forlorn, in total despair.

And Phil Tufnell was in the side. *Phil Tufnell*. He meant a lot to me at the time. A couple of summers previous, the voluntary 'cricket coach' at school phoned my house and asked my dad whether he knew that I bowled "lovely, loopy stuff", which of course he didn't. I mean, I didn't either. It was a total accident, I think I was trying to bowl as fast as I could in a game of Kwik Cricket. Yet as soon as I heard it, I felt like somehow it suited me.

Tufnell was, like me, a left-armer. He was bowling what resembled the loveliest, loopiest stuff you could ever imagine. His nickname was The Cat. He was obviously terrified of the ball. He batted 11. It was too much to be coincidence. I was the next Phil Tufnell in waiting. I read his book. It got better. Turns out you didn't really even need to try that hard to play for England, it just kind of happens. He visibly projected and promoted apathy and scruffiness. He smoked. He strolled around like even he wasn't taking it seriously.

When he came out to bat that day, he received a standing ovation. I absorbed it as a total celebration of character, acceptance of an outsider, a truly magic moment. He was the anti-gladiator. It's hard to explain to people now that the guy who desperately tries to fluff up Matt Dawson's jokes on *A Question of Sport* and occasionally does puff pieces about cats or old people on *The One Show* was my hero. But back then, he really was. He and anyone who played guitar.

It was the climax to a year in which cricket had quickly gathered momentum in my head. Earlier that summer, we'd gone to see Surrey play one-day cricket on a Wednesday afternoon. We told school we'd all caught the flu, probably off each other, "probably due to stress". The game was on Sky. Unbeknownst to us, there was Sky in the staff room. The ground was empty and we were the focal point of 'crowd' cutaways. I spent the next Wednesday evening locked in a classroom writing an essay on the importance of honesty. It didn't mention that I'd shouted "Ben!" at Ben Hollioake, who'd turned and smiled broadly back, and that the moment was worth a dozen detentions.

Naturally, it was the beginning of county cricket fan wildlife spotting, and it wasn't all roses. I can clearly recall things about

it I didn't like. I didn't like overhearing City boys in rugby shirts shouting "Cracking tits Jonesy", and I didn't like pavilion members looking over their shoulders and tutting and hissing at you. I still don't. It confused me about what liking cricket meant about me.

Sometimes I'm still not sure what the answer to that is. I was consoled, for the most part, that it was rare enough, and easily avoided. It served as the first warning of some of the confusing contradictions and peripherals in cricket that came with the territory. I'm not sure I really particularly loved people coming dressed as hot dogs in the name of fun either. Time though, has rendered them as comparatively harmless in my mind.

Meanwhile, my school cricket career was not going as I'd hoped. Even at 14, it was becoming clear that being a spinner that didn't spin it wasn't really going to work out, however much I reiterated to teammates that it was termed 'slow left-arm' for a reason. By the end of the season when I came on to bowl, the team instinctively and without instruction formed a ring on the outskirts of the boundary. It was kind of lovely, very loopy, and the already man-sized middle-order batsmen from schools in Kent teed off.

Music began to take over my life and I banked that; despite being pretty unlikely, it was a more realistic and less dangerous pipe dream. It transpired that what Phil Tufnell didn't mention in his book is that he was obviously naturally very, very good and always working harder than he let on. I suppose he had something that the greatest musicians possess: the ability to make something that has taken a lot of effort look effortless.

I don't know if I was aware of it at the time – from what I could gather we had always lost and always would do – but 1999 was a well-documented and necessary rebirth for English cricket. Darren Maddy, despite his outside-edge chasing-down efforts, wouldn't last much longer, but he will always have played his part in my head. Starting at the bottom is pretty liberating, and witnessing the nadir had set some kind of commitment in me that I knew was more than passing. So much so that when Nasser Hussain and Graham Thorpe chased down a Test series win in the pitch black in Karachi a year later, as much as it being their victory, somehow it felt a little bit like mine too.

Felix White is a musician, record label boss and co-host of the BBC's *Tailenders* podcast. His cricket-based memoir *It's Always Summer Somewhere* is out in 2021.

Phil Tufnell
evades a bouncer
from Dion Nash
at Lord's

ALAN GARDNER

2000

NEW MILLENNIUM, NEW ENGLAND

The coming of age of a revitalised England side who, inspired by their on-song pace quartet, defeated the Windies for the first time in more than 30 years

I was a football fan first. Where I grew up in mid-Essex during the 1990s, this was a popular move – like voting Tory, or watching *Noel's House Party*. There wasn't much cricket played at my secondary school, although back then it was at least a state comprehensive with *some* facilities. But the moustachioed sporting legend to be found on the posters in my bedroom was David Seaman rather than Graham Gooch.

We may worry now about how cricket competes against multiple forms of modern entertainment, but in some respects things weren't all that different back then. As a teenager, most days I was glued to a screen (in this case, the TV and Ceefax page 302), and there were plenty of other competing distractions. I had football, music, *Warhammer*, my PlayStation, the novels of Terry Pratchett... What did I need with another time-consuming, pocket money-draining, anorak-adjacent hobby?

My first really clear cricket memory is linked to the football. On Saturday, September 7, 1996, as Essex were plunging precipitously towards 57 all out in the NatWest Trophy final against Lancashire at Lord's, I was trudging to and from the clubhouse at the ground of my local non-league team, Heybridge Swifts, to give my dad updates on the score.

Essex's innings barely lasted until the final whistle. Goochie wouldn't be getting that spot on the wall. So began the gentle burble of background cricket that was to infiltrate my life over the next few summers. Dad took an interest, clearly, and the Test match would often be on when we

Craig White celebrates dismissing Brian Lara for a golden duck at The Oval

visited my grandparents on my mum's side. Their garden, with a handy concrete 'strip' up the middle and the back gate standing in for a wicket, was the arena in which my younger brother and I took it in turns to be Ronnie Irani. Pretty soon, *Brian Lara Cricket* was getting just as much use as the latest *FIFA*.

By 1999, I was ready to give over, if not my undivided attention, then at least a good chunk of my six-week holidays. But that was the year England managed to lose 2-1 at home to New Zealand, thus landing up bottom of the Wisden Test rankings. While I do hold fond memories of lying on the couch for the duration of Peter Such's 72-minute, 51-ball duck at Old Trafford (another Essex boy representin', innit), the fact Irani got a duff lbw decision in the Oval decider was always likely to sour things.

This was, I now know, good grounding for any neophyte England supporter. "Love in the nineties/Is paranoid," as Blur noted, albeit without any direct reference to the fear that the best efforts of Duncan Fletcher, Nasser Hussain and their predecessors were doomed to fail. Fortunately, with Y2K approaching, there was a real corker just around the corner.

The summer of 2000 was a coming of age story – both for me, and Nasser's boys. It was also the point at which cricket seemed to settle into its new surroundings on Channel 4, a year after switching from the Beeb, as Richie, Yozzer, Nicholas – a man whose florid, quasi-orgasmic commentary style almost seemed designed to trigger Proustian flashbacks – and the rest guided us through England's momentous tussle with the touring West Indians.

But first, let's get the season started in appropriate fashion, huddled in a corner of the County Ground for a Benson & Hedges Cup encounter between Essex and Hampshire. This wasn't my first match at Chelmsford, but it was Shane Warne's, as Hampshire's new overseas signing made his debut to no little fanfare – but not much of a crowd, given it was a Wednesday morning in April. Hampshire won the game, but Warnie's tepid figures of 0-44, which included being reverse-swept for four by Stephen Peters and thumped into the stands by Irani, was the bit that stuck with me.

And when I say stuck with me, I mean it was neatly recorded and filed away in my burgeoning collection of scorecards. It's all there, ready and waiting for the right eBay

Curtly Ambrose and Courtney Walsh leave the field together for the last time

buyer. In May, between GCSE exams and my 16th birthday, I nipped up to Chelmsford with my mate Alex for day four of a Championship match against Sussex (12.4 overs of play, then it rained); a week later, we got the train to Ilford, for the last first-class match ever played at Valentines Park. In July, it was a 45-over National League encounter against Middlesex, which the records show I scored every ball of. Did I mention not needing any more nerdy pastimes?

In truth, without such diligent jotting I don't think I would be able to recall much beyond the hazy sense of contentment those trips engendered. My most vivid memories came via the TV, flickering vignettes liveried in that distinctive orange and blue, and accompanied by the strains of Lou Bega.

The summer's marquee encounter was a rollicking affair, in many ways a precursor to 2005 and all that. West Indies may have been on the decline, but England had not managed to beat them in a Test series since 1969. Lara remained a mesmeric, kinetic force at the crease, while their bowling attack featured two all-time greats in harness. Ambrose and Walsh, Curtly and Courtney. Quentin Tarantino could not have come up with a more bad-ass pair, exuding menace and cool in equal measure. Ambrose was equipped with the stare of a basilisk, while Walsh was more likely to crack a grin – though if he did, it probably wasn't good news for you. Between them, they took 51 wickets and gave up four fifths of eff all.

Even the B-Movie bad guys, Reon King and Franklyn Rose, rose to the occasion as England were given a pasting in the first Test at Edgbaston. That might have been that, but this Hussain side had a bit of the "dogfuck" about them – to borrow the phrase Fletcher used to describe attack leader Darren Gough – and the second match produced a mongrel fightback of epic proportions (despite England missing their captain with a broken thumb). This game, for me, still sums up the unfathomable beauty of Test cricket. How could a team that had been crushed by an innings two weeks earlier, then shot out once again, produce such a turnaround, routing West Indies for 54 and then chasing 188 into the teeth of a Walsh six-for? But that is what happened, culminating in a spine-tingling afternoon at Lord's as Gough and Dominic Cork swindled the runs required, while me and my brother sat transfixed on the edge of our nan's hospital bed, trying not to jostle too excitedly (she was recovering from a hip replacement).

From four innings in one day, to four wickets in an over, the series set a thunderous pace. Lara's hundred saved West Indies at Old Trafford, where Marcus Trescothick made one of the most assured England debuts in decades. There were again shades of the 2005 Ashes here, as England left Manchester with a draw and a growing sense that the momentum was now with them. So it proved, as Andy Caddick's own mystic juju combined with the ley lines at Headingley and the see sawed definitively.

The final result was a rabble-rousing 3-1 win. At The Oval, where they had to shut the gates on the final morning, Mike Atherton scored his last Test hundred on home soil and England's quicks did the rest. Gough, Caddick, Cork and Craig White all averaged between 12 and 22 during the series. When White dispatched Lara for the first golden duck of his career, leg stump torpedoed as the great man swished like a drunken stevedore, I laughed, squealed and fell over all at the same time. I've never loved Test cricket more than when the bowlers have a sniff. That it was all there, filling the schedules on one of the five terrestrial channels, was simply [Benaud voice] "*Maaaarvelous*".

Looking back, this was a pretty cushty time to get on board. England were making history, Essex were winning promotion, and I'd been bitten by the millennium bug. That winter, Hussain led his team to famous wins in Pakistan and Sri Lanka – all of which I diligently followed via Ceefax page 341. Turns out I hadn't hit geek capacity (and probably never will).

I still like football, of course. It's a perfectly good way to warm up for the main event.

Alan Gardner is an associate editor at ESPNcricinfo and formerly of the Guardian.

GEOFF LEMON

2000/01

THE FIELD
IS SET

With West Indies' 2000/01 tour of Australia
went the last link to their golden era

t's a bright Australian afternoon, one of the last glowing embers of the year 2000. Jarvis Cocker has four days left to arrange a meeting with Deborah. Stanley Kubrick's spacecraft have 12 months to launch, and his isn't the only sci-fi title on the brink of anachronism. The day after Boxing Day, Australia's mediocre batting has been saved by Steve Waugh's century. West Indies walk out to reply.

The protagonists come in pairs. Sherwin Campbell and Daren Ganga. Glenn McGrath and Jason Gillespie. How the latter have tormented the former. This opening pair will never see another Test match, after eight innings averaging 10.06 runs each and 13.25 in partnership. Theirs is a microcosm of their team's struggle: over the preceding month West Indies have not only been taken apart, but stacked by the roadside and hauled off to the tip.

Campbell and Ganga cross the expanse of green, crowd poised to relish their failure. Fifteen years later, New Zealand will joke before a World Cup final that the MCG is so big that they'll get lost trying to find the pitch. On this day it looks that way – the batsmen hunched into tininess, Rick Moranis characters on a billiard table. The bowlers prance with equine assurance, high-stepping and mane-tossing. The field is set.

Slip. Slip. Slip. Slip. Slip. Gully. Gully.

Even seamer Andy Bichel is in the cordon. Now a short-leg, for the ball into the ribs: Justin Langer a metre from the batsman. Eight of nine available fieldsmen await a catch.

The only man not awaiting a catch is fine-leg, keeping the bouncer in play. The only man in front of the wicket is nobody. Melbourne's turf is a field of dreams. The merest defensive push will get you runs.

Steve Waugh's Australia line up at Sydney

Jason Gillespie bowls to a field of 10 catchers at the MCG

For seven overs, Campbell and Ganga do not score.

They flinch. They jump. They prod with bats angled and wrists askew. They leave innocuous ones, or bunt returns to sender. They are nerve bundles, jangling like a janitor's keys. They would have to join a marching band to spell this out any more blatantly. The bowlers groove a channel outside off. Each ball you hold your breath. The spell does not break. The batsmen are hypnotised. I will watch many better contests, but this will remain the most technically compelling passage of Test cricket I've seen.

I didn't know you were supposed to be afraid of the West Indies. As a television-minimal child of the 1980s, the Caribbean reign of joyful terror passed me by. So by 2000 I was able to feel sorry for them. The production line from Holding to Marshall to Ambrose had given way to Merv Dillon, Nixon McLean, Colin Stuart, Marlon Black. The batting was worse.

State sides cleaned them up in tour games. Australia's top three bowlers took 61 wickets at 17.90. I revelled in West Indies' smallest victories. It was a hammering, but god it was fun to watch.

Australia wore the Ansett logo, shortly before the airline's final landing. With an injured Shane Warne in the commentary box, McGrath got 11-27 in Brisbane, on a hat-trick twice before converting in Perth, where Brett Lee ran five through the tail. Colin Miller got 10 for the match in Adelaide, Andy Bichel his maiden five-for in Melbourne, where Gillespie had them 23-6 in the second. Stuart MacGill got seven in Sydney. Lower-order romps were in vogue, Adam Gilchrist often batting eight because of nightwatchmen. Lee and MacGill put on 50 in Brisbane and 48 unbeaten in Perth: 10.6 per cent of the leggie's career runs came in those knocks.

Miller, a club seamer turned offie, would soon be Australia's Test Player of the Year. He batted below MacGill in Adelaide and by Melbourne was pinch-hitting at six. I walked into the ground the second day to the roar of his hook over long-leg. Then emerging in Sydney with his hair dyed a peacock blue that sparkled in the sunlight, soon to become a sweat river down the back of his shirt. Federation Blue, he said with a grin, to the backdrop of Australia's centenary of colonial union. Courtney Walsh held up Miller's bowling for a laughter break after coming out to bat. *The Age* ran a glorious photo, the Footscray boy's arm around the giant Jamaican's back, both heads thrown back in mirth.

Walsh had a guard of honour in Sydney, and remains the highest wicket-taker between the sides. He entered the Gabba on one of McGrath's hat-trick balls only to charge the paceman and slice three over cover. The same approach avoided the follow-on in Melbourne, just, before he was run out in the excitement. He would play one more series, a late flurry against South Africa making him the first man past 500 Test wickets.

There was Lara's customary special, even in a struggling series. In Hobart against Australia A he came in at 80-5 and creamed 231, with six fours from one Bichel over. Then a straight surge into Adelaide, his cover-driven 182 all the more lavish because of the barren landscape in which it flowered. He made it known that he didn't rate MacGill: I think he hit four boundaries in an over and was dropped trying a fifth.

Ponting bowled too, red-cheeked and screaming at the umpire. Until his late-career statesmanship arrived, that piggy, spit-flecked visage was my image whenever his name arose. There was Marlon Samuels' debut, a slender elegant kid stroking 35 off 92 balls before coolly taking a couple of wickets that he didn't even celebrate. In a rice-paper team he was near miraculous.

There was the keeper, Ridley Jacobs, a proper tough operator who worked his guts out. Stranded on 96 in Perth when eight teammates made single figures. Equalling the record for catches in an innings. The once-dynamic captain Jimmy Adams played a doomed hero, his tour summed up by a backwards dive at mid-on, holding a brave catch before bashing his head and going off concussed. After the tour he would never play for West Indies again.

In Sydney, Campbell came good with twin fifties, new partner Wavell Hinds almost did the same, a young Ramnaresh Sarwan made 51 and the grinning leggie Mahendra Nagamootoo a hilarious 68. They still lost. Then Zimbabwe arrived for the ultimate daggy ODI tri-series: Doug Marillier's pioneering scoop shot when Zimbabwe missed Australia's 302 by a run; Ganga's one-stump run-out of Gilchrist from the square-leg fence; Damien Martyn's 144 as a temporary opener not enough to land the gig; Mark Waugh's Australian record of 173; Lara's hundred and a possible all-time great escape washed out at the SCG.

The West Indies never had another five-Test tour of Australia, and never will. With Walsh went the last link to the golden era. Lara remained, but quixotic genius in a failed side came to be more the mark of his career than an early association with the indomitable. That mantle would pass to Steve Waugh's team, who had just extended their streak of Test wins to 15. Two months later, they would travel to Mumbai for the 16th. What happened after that is most definitely another story.

Geoff Lemon is an Australian writer and broadcaster. His 2019 release *Steve Smith's Men* was named book of the year by *Wisden*, the Cricket Writers' Club and the Cricket Society/MCC. He is co-host of *The Final Word* podcast.

HENRY COWEN

2002

BUILDING SHRINES TO LIFE'S TRIERS

Forget the Queen's Golden Jubilee and remember instead her shaggy-haired subjects

Humans. We're all different. And that's a good thing. It's the same in cricket, it takes all sorts. Obdurate openers, elegant No.3s, talismanic all-rounders, podgy spinners, giant seamers and so on and so on – there's room for them all. For some of these cricketers, it's an easy game. Or at least it looks it. For others, it all seems to come a bit tougher. I don't know why, but I've always had a thing for 'the honest trier'. Those players who visibly give it everything they've got, as if cricket is a frustrating but ultimately rewarding chore. I've always been curious as to why this is and I think the reason might stem from the first Test match I watched live.

It was 2002, the football World Cup in Japan and South Korea had just started, the sun was out and – most importantly – the half-term holidays had just begun. It was

a good time. I remember finishing early on the Friday, my school had put on some horrific Richard Curtis-type event to celebrate the fact it was the Queen's Golden Jubilee. We had to dress as great Britons. I chose David Beckham, a shallow move on my part but an indicator that even then my fancy dress inspiration depended most on what clothes I already owned. I remember seeing my mum and her brilliant friend Carol doubled over in hysterics, to the extent they almost had to leave the school hall because they couldn't take the tawdry tweeness of the whole school singing *All You Need Is Love*. I was proud of them but happy to get away from the embarrassment of them making a scene.

The next day – with my mum probably still laughing – my dad, my brother and I drove up the Pershore Road towards Edgbaston. Having already been buoyed by Matt Holland, captain of my beloved and beleaguered Ipswich Town, scoring for Ireland against Cameroon, I should have realised it wasn't the kind of day you get to enjoy very often in your childhood. I mean, Matt Holland, at the World Cup!

The drive was one we used to take to head to Boundary Sports, the go-to cricket shop in the West Midlands. Trips there, with the promise of handling any number of bats, were exciting enough, but actually going to Edgbaston to watch England in a Test match? Excited doesn't even begin to cover it. It's a sad fact of life that the sense of awe you feel upon first entering a sporting arena is a once-in-a-lifetime thing: you'll never again be so amazed by the size, by the chatter, the expectation. We sat in the RES Wyatt Stand, much harder to see side-on, but it hardly mattered.

Sri Lanka were touring and England were on top. The visitors had been dismissed cheaply in the first innings and, in reply, Trescothick had scored a big hundred, which just seemed to be what happened as a matter of course. Things were set up nicely for the Saturday morning crowd: 401-5 with Thorpe and Flintoff ready to entertain. It wasn't to be, of course. Flintoff went earlyish and Alex Tudor, Ashley Giles and Andrew Caddick followed soon after. Muralitharan was doing what only he could do. I would have been very disappointed.

Out came Matthew Hoggard. I knew little of him, but I did know he wasn't very good at batting. In truth, those aliens watching cricket for the first time that we often muse about would have nudged each other and said: 'He's not up to much, is he?' It's the walk that gives him away. It's all lollop and no purpose, at the same time reluctant and dutiful. Thorpe was only on 61 – I wrongly remember him being much nearer his hundred – when he was joined by Hoggy. Work to be done.

From a spectator's point of view, this must have been a tad dry. Hoggy was good only for nose-to-the-ground blocks and while he played his card as well as ever, it's hard to believe it would have been as engrossing as I remember. The duo scored 92 runs in 30 overs, it's not pedestrian by any means but our man ended up unbeaten on 12, from 91 balls. Crucially, though, his efforts allowed Thorpe to reach his hundred. With his Chase bat wedged next to his Chase pad, everything unnatural and uncomfortable, Hoggard didn't let anything through. The team needed more runs, they always do, but what drove him on was the thought of his mate getting through to a hundred. That doesn't happen in other sports and it meant something.

It turned out to be a good time to start caring about cricket and the fortunes of the England team. The first Test I'd seen on TV was that classic victory over the West Indies two years

previously at Lord's – just imagine if my terrified No.11 had come out to hit the winning runs on that day, we'd have moved from admiration to full-blown love – and I was oblivious to England doing anything other than winning at home.

Later that summer England would play India. We would see Simon Jones' debut, Steve Harmison's debut, Rahul Dravid's excellence and *that* off-break by Michael Vaughan. There was the peculiarity of young Parthiv Patel, so young at 17 that technically he should have had written permission from his mum in order to not wear a helmet, there was the "fucking three!" brilliance from Nasser in the ODIs and that outlying Ajit Agarkar ton at Lord's. England's leading wicket-taker in the Tests was my man Hoggy, not that anybody realised.

If we accept the popular assertion that your first Test experience shapes your views on the game, then it's entertaining to imagine who and what has inspired what and why in cricket fans across the country. Is there a family home with a small shrine to Jon Lewis because they saw him clean up Michael Vandort at Trent Bridge in 2006? Might Usman Afzaal's enthusiastically celebrated dead-rubber half-century at The Oval in 2001 have won him some lifelong fans? And what repercussions – a question I often ask myself – did Rob Key's 221 at Lord's have on wider British society?

Fortunately for me, I backed a horse who went on to become one of England's finest bowlers. He has more wickets than any of the other fab four from '05, and he's the highest seamer on the list of English wicket-takers behind the three deadly duos of Anderson/Broad, Botham/Willis and Trueman/Statham.

Hoggard would go on to win the Man of the Match award at Edgbaston – his first in Tests – but it wasn't for his efforts with the bat. Indeed, those efforts had been eclipsed in the media by the death of Hansie Cronje, something which meant nothing to me. And given that the next day saw Sven-Göran Eriksson's England take on Sweden in their World Cup opener in Saitama, it's likely the back pages belonged to football and football alone. Such is life.

With Sri Lanka two wickets down on the Saturday evening we had left sunbeaten and happy. It had been as good as I wanted it to be. The next morning, befitting of a child who knew nothing of money, I begged my dad to let us return to Edgbaston to see day four: he gave in. Minus my brother, in bed recovering from sunstroke, it was just me and my old man. We sat in the Eric Hollies Stand. England won. Hoggard took five.

Henry Cowen worked at *All Out Cricket* magazine before becoming the media officer of the England Women's team.

Matthew Hoggard cleans up Sachin Tendulkar at Lord's

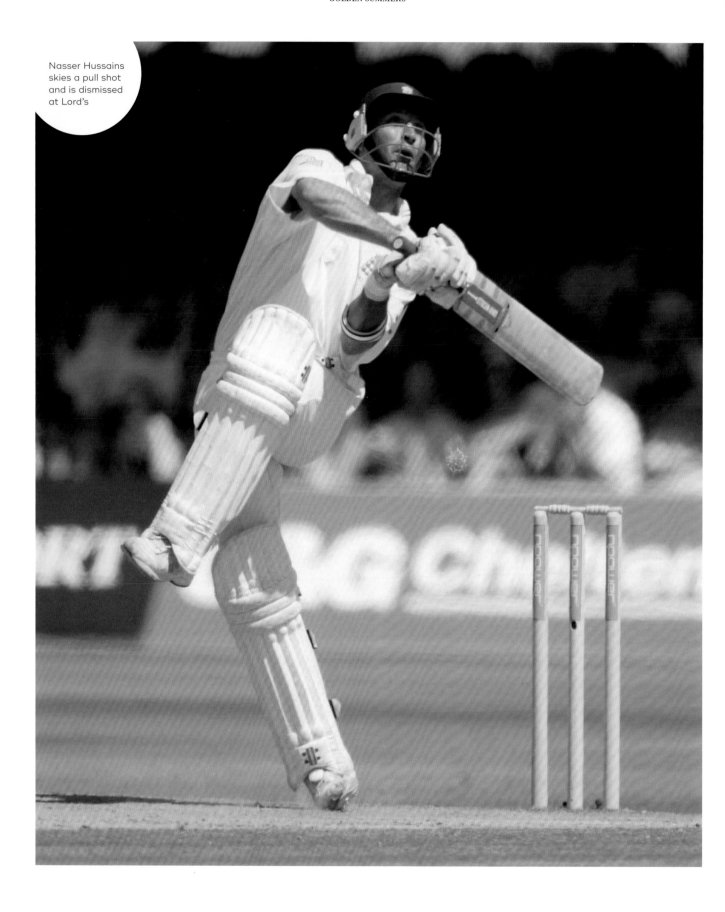

Nasser Hussains
skies a pull shot
and is dismissed
at Lord's

ED KEMP

2003

THE BLUE-AIRED DIN OF ADULT BATTLE

A transitional summer of heroes and hostility brought the fun back to playing for England

Mark Nicholas is leading me from the Lord's dressing room, talking right to me, walking me from the door of the home-team haven down the steps inside the pavilion. "This is where the new England captain Michael Vaughan will lead his players in just under an hour's time." To the ground floor – "You can easily get lost on this walk, many have" – round the corner, and into the Long Room, past the artefacts (animate and non), through the open doors and into daylight, down the steps and now, finally, onto the perfect green turf. Nicholas says something dramatic to camera and they throw to a montage. My teenage blood begins to sparkle.

What a way to start a broadcast on the first morning of a Test. And what a time: just turned 15, an endless summer holiday

ahead and a brand new England captain in office – all brought alive by the infectiously excited Channel 4 coverage.

It was 2003. Zimbabwe had come and gone away with two innings-defeats, South Africa had arrived led by a 22-year-old boy-giant we'd barely heard of, and form-wide under-performance in the end-of-year exams had delivered an unwelcome consignment of holiday Geography homework. A wonderful summer was tarnished only by the twin torments of Graeme Smith through mid-wicket and the complexities of longshore drift – natural phenomena as maddening and unremitting as each other.

A draw in the first Test at Edgbaston was laced with defeat: 338 runs had been scored before England took a wicket on the first day – one of relentless and dispiriting toil evoking the bleakest days of the '90s. My older brother and I – idle sofa partners for England matches throughout these years – shared custody of a cricket ball during the hours of play, taking turns in buffing one side to a perfect sheen (and even, I'll admit, scuffing up the other). There's little to compare to the joy of a well-shined cricket ball, and, by the close on that first day, we probably had more to show for our efforts than England did.

South Africa's monstrously bottom-handed young skipper ("what's-his-name", as Nasser Hussain had regrettably referred to him pre-series) had mercilessly bludgeoned 277. Though a whole day of rain – and a wonderful hundred by run-machine Michael Vaughan – helped England avoid defeat, the game brought about the resignation as captain of my beloved Nasser. Smith, not for the last time, was heaping on the pain.

So, Lord's. Just two days later. Vaughan had been captaining a newly invigorated one-day side who had just won the ODI tri-series. Nasser, who'd seemed a tired old dog reverting to his well-worn tricks in Birmingham – the Freddie-round-the-wicket, the Gilo-at-the-legs, the misfield bollockings – felt like it was no longer his team. Watching him fall back into the ranks that summer was infinitely analysable to detail-hungry cricket nerds like us. Diminished in stature and under pressure for runs as never before, he reacted in the only way he knew: scrapping away with a lion heart and a potty mouth.

With existing pretensions as an opening bat and captain myself, I was naturally drawn to a) any England captain and b) battling batsmen of the ticker-and-temperament variety. I was also a couple of years in to my induction in men's league cricket and was, far from turned off by its lack of gentility, utterly enthralled by it: the blue-aired din of *adult* battle. People didn't seem to think cricket was a tough game, but I knew different. They also disliked swearing, but they were wrong about that, too. As far as I was concerned swearing was big, clever and very fucking satisfying indeed. And in that I'd had Nasser's England to prove me right.

A few moments from that second Test at Lord's stick out: with England having collapsed for 173 on the first morning (it was, incidentally, the beginning of a terminal decline in Vaughan's own batting powers), Nasser was moved from his former home at mid-on/mid-off to a short cover position, where he promptly dropped Smith on 8. How on earth he must have been feeling as Upstart Biff went on to make 259 – a second double hundred in successive Tests. Later, Smith (whose side Nasser had claimed were "ripe for the taking" ahead of the Tests) was at the non-striker's end with a 21-year-old James Anderson bowling, and began to draw the umpire's attention to Anderson's follow-through. Nasser jumped in with a volley telling Smith to mind his own.

I would hoover up more minutiae a year later when Ed Smith published his diary of the season, *On and Off the Field*. Smith had been the standout batsman in county cricket that summer and made a debut in the third Test at Trent Bridge in place of Anthony McGrath. I always so wanted debutants to do well, and he did – making fifty in Nottingham before missing out on selection for the winter tour to conclude a three-Test international career. Smith wrote how his first innings began as Nasser's partner, and when short-leg fielder Paul Adams began chirping the new man, Nasser (who would go on to make a meaningful hundred)

marched down the track to make the fight his own with a simple: "Fuck off, Adams." If Vaughan's takeover heralded a reduction in tongue-lashings for the England team themselves, that didn't have to mean the opposition wouldn't still taste a bit.

Nasser's harshest words were perhaps reserved for himself, though. In the fourth innings at Lord's, with England attempting to bat out for a draw (his home turf), he made it to 61 before attempting a weird, wrist-flapping pull from outside off to Makhaya Ntini. As the ball lobbed up for a simple catch to Mark Boucher, Nasser let out a desperate, self-loathing roar that still hurts a little to think about. It all just meant so much.

The drama was in presentation as well as content. When former captain Hussain had joined new captain Vaughan at the crease on that first morning at Lord's, Nicholas had buzzed on commentary that it was "a fascinating juxtaposition". I remember it so clearly: there was Nicholas, with his innocent enthusiasm for the spectacle, and Nasser, with that unpasteurised passion for the contest. They were very different men but both had long won me over. They seemed to love cricket as much as I did.

Change was afoot, though. Our ball well burnished, my brother deserted at the end of that summer (something about going to university) and I, oxbow-laked up to the eyeballs, would be setting about my GCSEs. England, meanwhile, were quickly getting better and better at cricket.

Despite the uncertain start (England lost by an innings and 92 at Lord's, and their injury-hit attack in the fourth Test at Headingley was spearheaded by James Kirtley, Martin Bicknell and Kabir Ali) Vaughan grew a team unshackled by the kind of intensity Nasser had so successfully and, at the time, necessarily delivered. Perhaps it even started in that failed match-saver at HQ: with the game gone, an ever-improving Andrew Flintoff had some fun in the second innings, smashing 142 and hitting Ntini (who later broke Flintoff's Woodworm bat) for an unforgettable straight six into the pavilion. England won the third and fifth matches to secure a battling 2-2 draw, with Graham Thorpe making a memorable comeback century and Marcus Trescothick compiling a monumental 219 in the final game at The Oval. The following summer, after a career defined by struggle, Hussain got the uncomplicatedly glorious sign-off he deserved. Only one year on from *that*, 2005 happened.

Yes, things changed. Channel 4's rights wouldn't last forever and neither did Nicholas' status as the foremost anchor-commentator. My own tastes there and elsewhere moved on, as did my attitude to on-field aggression; my view on *how cricket should be played* completed a gradual about-turn 10 years later. But back in 2003, when grown men were trying (unnecessarily) to talk me out, an intrepid Mark Nicholas was wafting along the front line with a camera crew in tow, and a battle-scarred Nasser Hussain was shouting at anything that moved. Cricket was pure, intoxicating combat. And I absolutely loved it.

Ed Kemp was a writer at *All Out Cricket* magazine and *wisden.com* before thinking better of it.

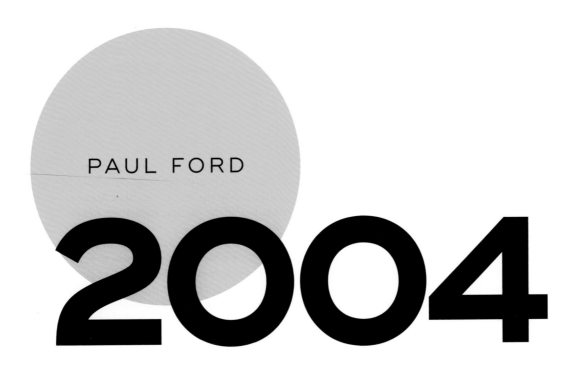

PAUL FORD

2004

THE SWEET TASTE
OF DEFEAT

An overseas cricket tour is never about winning,
else no one would do it…

I n 2004 this New Zealand-born, Wellington-dwelling, near-obsessive Kiwi cricket fan fell in love with England. Not her slimy fish and chips and grimy peas, nor her warm beer or black cabs and buskers, nor her surprisingly good weather and certainly not London's pomp and ceremony. No, I fell in love with her cricket.

When I walked through those gates at Lord's, after travelling 18,813km from The Land of the Long White Cloud, I was preposterously excited.

Straight off the plane, a bag drop in Shepherd's Bush, a beer and brekkie down the gizzard at the Lord's Tavern and there, in NW8, my golden summer began. I was leading the Beige Brigade's first northern hemisphere foray and we would see every ball of the three Test matches. A season opener at Lord's was the ultimate way to begin.

The citadel of cricket in St John's Wood lures lovers of leather on willow like dopey moths to a flickering flame. It feels and sounds like a religious spot, despite being named after a bloke called Thomas.

We queued up, our ironic brown-and-tan uniforms clashing with the bacon-and-egg garb of the members, yet blending in with a disturbing number of other punters dressed in beige for no good reason. The strains of a Maori waiata rang out across the Nursery Ground as we climbed the steps, aiming for the front row of the Upper Edrich Stand.

A resplendently green-blazered steward called Adam came and greeted us and reminded us of the rules on his patch. These included sensible things such as making sure we only brought in one bottle of wine each, limited our walkabouts to in-between overs, and didn't curse too loudly when New Zealand lost a wicket. He finished with: "If there's anything I can do to help you out today, please don't hesitate to pop up and see me." Extraordinary.

I loved seeing all 163cm of the Old Father Time weather vane atop the Mound Stand, placidly removing the bails from the stumps, and his hat-tip to Law 16(3). I loved the slope, and the way everyone bangs on about this 180cm undulation intermittently for five days. I loved being able to buy a bucketload of Pimm's – for the deposit on a four-bedroom house in New Zealand – furnished in a jug jam-packed with cucumber, strawberries, fizz and happiness.

We dreamed of a magnificent victory, like the one culminating with a match-winning leg-side squirt for four by Matthew Bell in 1999. Chris Cairns was sensational with the ball: who could forget that loopy slow yorker to a curled-up Chris Read?

But then the cricket happened.

This was the match that began the Test career of Andrew Strauss, who scored 112 and 83, and gave Nasser Hussain the opportunity to bid farewell with a frustrating, emotional, match-winning 103 in a near-perfect second-innings run chase of 282.

We loved the obstinate batting of Mark Richardson, whose 93 and 101 "filled the bars" according to English journalist Mike Walters. We hated the agonising 96 from our makeshift No.3 Brendon McCullum, the young tyro of Kiwi cricket at the time.

And of course we will never forget the batting of Chris Cairns – walloping Jones, Harmison and Flintoff into the stands as he went past Viv's record of 84 sixes in Test cricket. His 82 from 47 balls was a thrilling assault on the English bowlers – unadulterated power accompanied by smiles, bewildered head-shaking and a massive standing ovation.

Headingley is a brilliant cricket ground, but provided us with a massive culture shock after the poshness of NW8. No bacon-and-egg ties here, no Pimm's. Adam was replaced by burly fluoro-vested security guards with wrestler beards and policemen with video cameras.

The grimy Yorkshire skies chucked it down on day one, so we found – then lost – our bearings in the million pubs within a cooee of the ground. Our Fawlty Towers-style accommodation backed onto the perimeter fence of the ground so we could come and go with reckless abandon.

Not many Kiwis made the journey up north, as we found out when we landed at Yeadon after a European jaunt between matches. I was confronted by an immigration official: "What, cricket? This is roogby layg country, boyo," said the uniform suspiciously.

Of course once you get closer to this legendary ground, with its tales of Botham's heroics, Dickie Bird's yarns and Boycott's curmudgeonry, it is the only show in town. It's also one of two places in England where you hear banter about 15th-century

history in between overs, as the War of the Roses is relitigated with visiting Lancastrians.

Dress-up day on the Western Terrace is manna from heaven for the local costume-hire shop: monks, sailors, babies, smurfs, at least seven dwarves, pilots, sheep, Star Wars, hobbits, Baywatch babes, nuns, lifeguards, Marios, Playboy bunnies and a man who looked like Claudio Ranieri were all there. We applauded the WWF-style confrontations between Hulk Hogan, The Ultimate Warrior, Wetsuit Man and Saddam Hussein. We partook in the clandestine tearing up of the *Daily Telegraph's* freely distributed sports section, arising en masse with the rest of the terrace in a slow Mexican wave to play our part in one of the greatest scatterings of newspaper confetti in global history.

Again, the atmosphere overshadowed the action on the field, at least from a New Zealand perspective. In amongst the beer-snake construction and the endless Anglo-Kiwi banter, there were very few cricketing highlights, with injuries to Papps, Vettori and Oram stealing the show.

When Trescothick and Strauss knocked up a partnership of 150-plus for the first wicket, it was the beginning of desperate times. We headed back to Fawlty Towers and donned our crotch-hugging lycra suits to create our own fun and distract attention from the on-field pain.

It didn't work. Harmison and Hoggard were wonderful and deservedly picked up 13 wickets between them, and the supposedly hopeless new wicketkeeper Geraint Jones pummelled a cut-laden maiden Test century. We'd had a great week in Leeds but we headed to the Midlands with any chance of a series win extinguished.

We started our visit to Nottingham with a wonderful tour of the Gunn & Moore factory, followed by a session on Trent Bridge history with the in-ground historian. The history was rich too, this being the English home away from home for a long line of Kiwi cricketers including Hadlee, Astle, Cairns and Fleming.

We wandered to the middle of the ground to investigate the New Zealand team's net session and assess the pitch – incredible access given the Test was due to start the next day – and celebrated with 100 beers and 100 chicken wings with the GM crew at Hooters.

This was the closest match of the series, with New Zealand holding the early ascendancy as Stephen Fleming and Scott Styris piled on the runs on day one: at 272-2 we dared to dream again. But England kept in touch and bowled brilliantly in the second innings, with Wheelie-bin Giles in his punishing sunglasses grabbing four wickets with innocuous spin.

The target of 284 was England's fifth-highest successful run chase of all time, despite a valiant effort from Cairns, who snared nine wickets in his final Test. Graham Thorpe led the way with the bat, hitting a typically gritty 104 to snaffle a third win.

Away from the stands, we'd loved life in Nottingham. One memorable evening we revisited the pints and wings of Hooters then found ourselves leading a glorious singalong to Hey Jude, having just lost a boat race to a bunch of English fans dressed as Coronation Street stars. It was peak England.

The final memory of the series was the sight of the slowest members of their respective squads – Giles and Richardson – in an end-of-series sprint around the outfield. New Zealand had finally won something.

If there is ever a time to test whether you're a patriot or a cricket lover, it is in the midst of a 3-0 Test series shellacking. And in England's green and pleasant land we realised that we were definitely the latter, and we were definitely not alone.

Paul Ford is *Wisden Cricket Monthly*'s New Zealand correspondent and co-founder of the Beige Brigade, New Zealand's supporters' group.

Mark Richardson and Ashley Giles do battle at Trent Bridge

TIM KEY

2005

THE
BIG ONE

*England hadn't beaten Australia in 18 years; who thought this
would be any different?*

ou think I'm not nervous writing about
the 2005 Ashes? You think I don't
understand the responsibility?

If you're over 50 there *is* another
contender. Of course there is. You've
got Botham, 1981 and all that: players
checking out of hotels early, olden-
days folk listening to the wireless in traffic jams, Willis' locks
steaming in, Botham's huge arms, Botham's sixes, Botham's cigar.
Botham. If you're under 15, then fair play, you're all about Stokes
and Leach, and good luck to you. Anything in between though
and there's only one summer for you: 2005. No ifs. No buts. And
my experience of it, as a rookie comedian, was as follows.

When you're a cricket fan, your summer is defined by the Test
match itinerary. Similarly, when you're a young comedian, your
summer is defined by the Edinburgh Fringe Festival. When

you're both, things get blurry. August starts to stretch, quite
palpably, at the seams. It squeaks. If it's an Ashes summer, the
problem becomes bigger. And if it's the greatest Ashes contest of
all time, you're done for.

I was there with my sketch group. We were called Cowards
and comprised four men, two of whom wore blue shirts and
two of whom wore pink. Doesn't sound great, but listen, we
sold out our *52-seater* most days, so we were doing something
right. Lean and mean, we were a four-pronged attack. Flintoff,
Harmison, Hoggard and Jones, if you will. We all knew our
jobs. We wanted it. To say we were fired up when we arrived
at Waverley Station barely covers it. Off the train, heaving the
stench of hops into our lungs, marching to our digs. Cup of tea.
Channel 4 *on*. Roll *Mambo No.5*.

The first Test was already done and dusted by the time we'd
left London. Ashley Giles was still being compared to a wheelie

Michael Vaughan reclaims the urn for England after 18 years of hurt

bin as we unpacked our understated props. A chef's hat here, a tutu there. I had somehow snared tickets to the final Test at The Oval but that just made me feel sick. That rubber was already looking dead as ice-cold catfish. McGrath had sliced us apart at Lord's. We were done for. Rolled over by an Australia at the top of its game. No one wanted to say it, but this had 5-0 written all over it. I say no one. McGrath said it a bit, if asked. England had dropped Graham Thorpe, brought in a tall South African with a white bit in his hair. We'd been outplayed. We eyed up Edgbaston nervously. August looked grim. A bleak atmosphere cloaked our technical rehearsal. And yet...

Four days later, we'd won the second Test and all was rosy again. I say won – we still had to clean up a couple of wickets on the final morning, but, yeah, basically won. The festival was in full swing by then and we were bleary-eyed as we peeled ourselves out of bed and settled in to watch the remaining Aussies get knocked over. After that we would set to work, tweaking our jokes, honing our timing. But, half an hour in and Brett Lee's prodding had turned to occasional whacking, and we shut the hell up. We listened to Richie. We drank coffee. We prayed. Did everything we could to will a wicket. People facing the wrong way on sofas, our director making toast and bellowing, TV off, TV back on. It felt like our whole month depended on that morning. Kasprowicz hits the winning runs, we might as well go home now. His stumps get crushed, we win the Perrier. Our destiny dangled by a thread in Birmingham. And then, finally, Flintoff's on his haunches, giving Lee a nice pat on the helmet and our month is up and running.

It's sad to think that this series was Test cricket's last big terrestrial TV moment. It's sad they threw that away. Everyone was at cricket's altar that morning. Praying silently into the free-to-air air. Cricket on Channel 4, what a gift. But of course we couldn't be sat in front of every ball. We had a sketch show to perform each day at 4.45pm. On the stroke of tea we'd meet in the Pleasance Courtyard, the spiritual epicentre of the fringe. Breeno, our director – a kind of Liverpudlian Duncan Fletcher – would sit the four of us round a picnic table. And as the Zimbabwean Fletcher rounded on his four, herculean fast bowlers, so our one piled into us. Probably the same notes, too. Quicker! More accurate! Discipline! Those people have paid to see you! Be brave! Hold a good length, Gilchrist'll lose patience! I'd like to say that my mind was on the show. I'd love to. But

you try focusing on a sketch about a magic hat when you know England have just lost Trescothick cheaply and Gillespie's got his dander up.

The glorious narrative of the Test series put our 55-minute show to shame. For us it was a selection of 18 three-minute sketches. They were knitted together by blackouts and covered the core themes of beekeeping, hot-air balloons and Sir Steven Redgrave. No ambitious overarching themes. No simmering subtext. Zero backstory. Back in England stories emerged and interwove. McGrath – thank God – trod on a cricket ball. Flintoff was having 'duels'. It ebbed, it flowed, we picked off sessions where we could.

I was watching Mark Watson's epic '24-hour show' as Ponting dug in to save the Old Trafford Test, asking for scores, bemoaning Punter, involuntarily playing hook shots. It sounds disrespectful to Mark, but believe me, he was keeping across it, too. When Ashley Giles threw off his wheelie bin to win at Trent Bridge, I was in some squalid performers bar, stood with other addled comedians, living every forward press, cheering every run. Older, wiser comedians invested in portable transistor radios. You peered at scorecards through windows. The safest thing though was not to leave the flat. The city was flooded with comedians that summer – your Tim Vines, your Miranda Harts, your Ross Nobles – and I'm sure they were fantastic. But, to be fair, I wouldn't know. And I have *zero* regrets about watching 400 Simon Jones deliveries that month while eating Tunnock's in a high-ceilinged lounge.

Edinburgh finished. I arrived at The Oval with us 2-1 up. For me though, this is a footnote. I loved watching KP swatting 158 as if he were clearing his kitchen of wasps. I loved seeing 'Warney' fumble the ball to the ground, logging it there and then as my 'I was there' anecdote for any dinner parties I might get the nod for. I loved nervously squeezing my plastic pint glass as Paul Collingwood MBE put together his 10. On paper, that should have been the highlight of my summer. But the highlight was something different. It was the way in which Tests #two to #four spread like custard through my Edinburgh that will stay with me forever. The greatest sporting summer bar none, hundreds of miles away from the action, catching it when I could. Cricket was sliding in between the crevices and, unlike 'Warney', any chance I got, I took it.

Tim Key is a comedian, actor, poet and deep-lying playmaker.

DEAN WILSON

2008

THE MAN WHO FELL TO EARTH

A mercurial outsider taking hold of English cricket; it could never last, but what a show it was

What was so special about 2008? Well, if you live in the real world and are not obsessed by cricket like me then you might mumble something about the global financial crisis, or the election of Barack Obama as the 44th President of the United States of America. Worthy subjects sure, but in the bubble of English cricket 2008 will always be the year of change that split the successful eras of Michael Vaughan and Andrew Strauss.

Let's call it the year of the KP.

It was a midpoint four years after Kevin Pietersen's England debut and six years before his international career came to a juddering halt. Even though cricket is a team game, his career arc is a thing of perplexing beauty.

There have been other players during this period who have done incredible things and made huge contributions, but for the 10 years that Pietersen was an England player, no man had a greater influence or polarised opinion more than he did, and I found it utterly fascinating.

It was my sixth summer covering the England team but my second as the *Daily Mirror* correspondent. There was no hint of the jaded hack, I was still full of youthful enthusiasm about the team I was following, and as the summer began to unfurl, there was a genuine hope that Pietersen might just take England singing and dancing into another glorious period of success. At least that is how it looked at the time. I was still buzzing from the tour to New Zealand when I reported for duty back at Lord's for the first Test of the summer.

It truly is the most stunning country and a joy to visit, especially when you can cover almost all of it by road amid the scenery. So when the warm and friendly Kiwis arrived in the UK for round two, it almost felt like the tour had simply continued.

Maybe I was in a sauvignon blanc inspired perma-haze which is why I remember it so fondly, but it was just a happy time. I had moved in with my girlfriend, now wife, and I was doing a job that I loved deeply. The seeds had been sown by my Bajan father many years ago and it felt like I was reaping the benefits.

Just a few weeks earlier Brendon McCullum had swapped me a tennis racket for a beer fridge after a golf tournament near Christchurch, on the basis that I might struggle to get the beer fridge in my luggage, and he made a point of shouting me a couple of frosty ones when we met in a bar in Manchester ahead of the second Test. Life was good.

I felt like I belonged and I was part of something cool, and the way Pietersen played the game was a big part of that. He made the game fun and entertaining. Cricket seemed less stuffy when KP was involved and that was a good thing.

England went on to win the next two matches to take the series with Pietersen scoring a match-winning 115 at Trent Bridge.

He had of course given us all a taste of his outrageous talent – be it on his debut one-day tour to Zimbabwe and South Africa in front of a hostile crowd, or at The Oval in the 2005 Ashes which announced him as a superstar, and in 2006 he first unveiled the soon-to-be-patented switch-hit, taking on Muttiah Muralitharan in a way that no England player had ever previously dared.

And yet in 2008 he produced two shots that were to stun the opposition, the crowd and all those watching on TV in a way that only he could.

The image of Pietersen, not once but twice, switch-hitting Scott Styris over cow-corner – or was it extra cover? – for monstrous sixes has become part of cricket folklore, as too the response from the bowler. A scratch of the chin, a rueful smile and the knowledge that he had not only been beaten, but he had been scarred. This was life-affirming stuff.

By the time the Test series against South Africa came around Pietersen was batting as well as he ever had and it showed with a brilliant 152 at Lord's, his first Test against his country of birth. It must have been a bizarre but exhilarating feeling for him.

Pietersen, who loves South Africa the place to his core, but feels spurned enough to move abroad and try and make a go of cricket elsewhere. He finds it hard to reconcile the decision he has made so he lashes out and engages in a war of words with the likes of Graeme Smith over the issue, calling him an "absolute muppet". It is why he is so reviled when he goes back for the first time and is booed to high heaven. He takes it and responds this time with the bat and not the mouth.

Now here he is at the home of cricket, the place where you make history, and he is doing it against the team he would have hoped to have played for a few years previously.

It is this sense of identity that fascinates me, in the way that you'd expect as the son of West Indian parents who taught me to cheer on the Windies, but who cheered on England against every other team. Torn loyalties that become a win-win because you can't lose!

As the world gets smaller it becomes increasingly difficult to be certain of your identity if you or your family moves from one place to another, and yet it is that firm idea of who you are and where you come from that enables you to find your way in somewhere new.

I guess it's hard enough trying to live and work in a new land when no one is watching, let alone when you're doing it in front of thousands studying your every move. And yet it is out in the middle in the heat of the battle where Pietersen was most at home and felt most secure. It was all so simple in the middle, you just had to score runs and that is all you're judged on.

Off the field you're judged on what you look like, what you sound like, where you're from, who you know and who you don't know. You are pre-judged.

The series continued with Smith and his team dominating at Leeds in what we shall call the 'Pattinson Affair' and then again at Edgbaston when Pietersen holes out for 94 and ends an innings that, had it continued another few overs, may well have set up a win. At 2-0 down with one to play the series was over and so too was Vaughan's captaincy.

Enter stage left the new captain of England in every format going. The outsider was now at the helm of the establishment and promising to do it his way. I was swept along by his positive messages before the final Test at The Oval and had begun to think that perhaps this single-minded, selfish player would use those traits for the good of the team. He talks a good game, and he plays a good game, scoring a hundred in a six-wicket win, but that is as good as it gets.

A terrorism-influenced tour to India later and it is all over. He is stripped of the captaincy while Peter Moores is sacked as coach. A huge schism opens up between Pietersen and the ECB which is never closed.

I think Pietersen actually had his happiest moment as an England player in 2008, as captain raising his bat for that hundred against South Africa at The Oval. It certainly looked that way to me. I know I had a great time watching it.

Dean Wilson is cricket correspondent of the *Daily Mirror*.

Kevin Pietersen does the unthinkable and switch-hits Scott Styris for six

ISABELLE
WESTBURY

2009

STEPPING INTO
THE VOID

*A summer which marked a turning point in cricket's
balance of power*

ot many people will have heard of Tim de Leede. Fewer will count him among their first cricketing heroes. But he was mine. Owner of a sports shop by day, destroyer of international cricketing giants in his spare time, the powerful all-rounder was the embodiment of Dutch amateur cricket in the Noughties, of a nation scrapping to compete in an increasingly professional world.

By 2009, with de Leede two-years retired and cricket slipping lower down the Dutch sporting agenda, the Netherlands were pitted against England as the rankest of outsiders for the opening game of the World T20 at Lord's. England were expected to launch the tournament in an explosion of six-hitting and athleticism, demonstrating the thrill of T20 cricket. What we got was more dramatic than anything anticipated, just not in the way expected.

We knew that T20 cricket was fast-paced, exciting and capable of attracting a new breed of fan; what wasn't necessarily factored in was just how unpredictable it could be. The Netherlands' final-ball victory over the hosts, a scrambled run to an overthrow, showed its potential for giant-killing.

"It wasn't quite the butcher, baker and candlestick-maker, but it was the repo man, the restaurateur and the insurance broker who embarrassed England in an astonishing start to the World Twenty20," wrote Mike Atherton in *The Times*. "This was the greatest night in Dutch cricketing history – and one of England's worst."

De Leede might not have been there, but his legacy of the underdog amateur was. The Netherlands had beaten England before, in 1989 and 1993, but that was a different age, when the gulf between amateur and professional cricket was not so vast. It had grown exponentially since. The advent of T20, however,

Ryan ten Doeschate steers the Netherlands to a shock win over England

GOLDEN SUMMERS

suddenly provided a means to close that gap, if only fleetingly. The Netherlands would beat England again in their next and only T20 encounter since, in 2014. In this format they have a 100 per cent record against England.

While the IPL had started the previous year and the first World T20 a year before that, this was perhaps the first time the format was taken seriously in its own right; to host both the men's and women's final at Lord's was momentous.

India, so often the country to which work is outsourced, had reversed this by effectively outsourcing the lucrative IPL to South Africa earlier in 2009 following security concerns at home. A new world order had been born.

The tournament was such a success that the biggest news story ahead of England's home Test series against West Indies was that Chris Gayle had the gall to turn up only two days before the first match, having come straight from the IPL.

A s an expat English kid introduced to cricket on the volatile coconut matting of Dutch football-cum-cricket grounds, 2009 also marked a turning point in my own relationship with the game. While I revelled in the triumph of the Dutch, that summer I became English. Having represented the Netherlands based on residency qualifications as a young teenager, when I moved back to England in 2007 I joined Somerset – but as their overseas player. Never has a resident overseas possessed quite such a plummy accent, nor likely been quite as underwhelming a player. Justin Langer, then playing for Somerset men, I was not. It meant that any ambitions to represent England had been put on hold, at least until 2009.

Come that summer I was now English, and England Women had just done the double: a World Cup win in Australia and the World T20 title at Lord's. Just as female enfranchisement in 1918 was attributed to women filling the factory workers' void where men could not, so England's women cricketers were filling a trophy cabinet that the men had yet to touch.

It was my chance to stake a claim for a place in this coveted England set-up. I felt ready. The cricketing gods, however, were not. After a broken arm in pre-season and county batting and bowling averages that would have satisfied most had they been reversed, by the time the Ashes arrived in early July, any early aspirations of improving my international average of nought were looking remote.

As the men's first Ashes Test drew to its dramatic close in Cardiff, the match-saving exploits of Jimmy Anderson and Monty Panesar offered some hope that batting was a skill even the most unlikely might be able to, if not master, at least improve upon. Still, the mood in the car was a solemn one as I joined my Somerset teammate, the then 17-year-old Anya Shrubsole, with her father Ian on a day-trip to watch the women's Ashes Test at New Road. While I was quietly contemplating my own life choices, Anya, already a World Cup winner, was seething at not having been picked for the Test.

The outrage, the emotion, the teenage fragility – I'm still not sure how Ian survived that journey.

The match itself hardly even registers. It would be the last women's Ashes series in England to be decided in this arcane manner – one Test between the two nations whose fixture list featured barely one long-form international match per year. As the game petered out to a draw, what was more significant was that this result, England retaining the Ashes as winners of the previous bout, meant they reigned supreme as holders of all major titles available to them.

Such global dominance – with their talismanic captain Charlotte Edwards leading the way on the field and Clare Connor, the ECB head of women's cricket, equally driven off it – was unprecedented. This team would become the cornerstone of a new era of women's cricket, from which a fully professional game has emerged. The New Road Test may not have had much of an immediate impact, but something must have clicked. Come August, with a disappointing county season behind me but with England's men in the midst of an enthralling Ashes series, finely poised at 1-1 after Australia's bounce-back at Headingley, anything seemed possible. I was named captain of one of the four teams competing in the Junior Super Fours, an under 19 competition featuring the best young players in the country. I finished as the tournament's leading run-scorer and wicket-taker, hitting an unbeaten century in the final which featured several dropped catches and a wagon-wheel with a magnet seemingly stationed at square-leg.

Recently there has been much conjecture surrounding the rationale of favouring young cricketers, brimming with potential, over seasoned, proven stalwarts in international and first-class selections. I was one of those upstarts. Propelled into the England Academy on the back of a season where the stats couldn't have been more contrasting – flourishing in age-group cricket, floundering on the county circuit – mine was a brief stint at the top.

If, on a personal level, 2009 started in frustration but ended in triumph, the same could be said of another young cricketer who would go on to enjoy a far more successful international career. The abiding image of England's defeat to the Netherlands was of a disconsolate Stuart Broad, head in hands in disbelief. Fast forward two months and Broad's five-for, including a golden spell of four wickets for eight runs, saw him crowned Man of the Match in the series decider at The Oval. It was to be the start of Broad's love affair with the Ashes and I, for one, was hooked.

It was a summer of hope – some of it later fulfilled, other bits less so – which proved that cricket, despite its fusty image, could and would change. It was now just a matter of how far and how fast.

Isabelle Westbury is a writer for the *Telegraph* and *Wisden Cricket Monthly* and a former captain of Middlesex Women.

154

Charlotte Edwards' team won the inaugural Women's World T20

King Kumar: Sangakkara is taken for a lap of honour after the World T20 final

ANDREW FIDEL
FERNANDO

2014

THE EIGHT-MONTH PARTY

Over a few crazy months the Sri Lanka cricket team freewheeled to a ludicrous World T20 win and a series victory in England

A ball-tampering controversy, frenetic last-session chases, two consecutive final-over Test finishes, captaincy meltdowns, masterly spin from Rangana Herath, searing reverse-swing from Dale Steyn – the first eight months of Sri Lanka's 2014 were so high-octane just in the Test format, you almost forget they had won a World T20 and an Asia Cup in between.

This was the season in which Sri Lanka conjured beauty from chaos, their stars aligning, galaxies colliding together, the team charging through the year with a frenzied, unpredictable energy – ionised matter shooting through an asteroid field. There were many triumphs but also haunting lows. No game was short of a twist.

In those months, they had the talent of raising unmissable drama even from the most humdrum situations. In the first series

of the year, against Pakistan in the UAE, Sri Lanka went into the third Test at Sharjah 1-0 up in the series, and spent much of the match essentially trying to draw it, playing out four dreary, eventless days. It appeared as if Sri Lanka would succeed in defending their series lead when they began the final day 220 runs ahead and with five wickets in hand, but of course they collapsed, leaving Pakistan 302 to get with 59 overs to score them in.

Azhar Ali, generally among the more dour of Pakistan's batsmen, was suddenly transformed in the final innings of the series, as if he had drunk some strokemaking elixir. Even as Sri Lanka's captain Angelo Mathews put men on the boundary and instructed his attack to fire deliveries down the leg-side, Azhar sent Pakistan skating towards their target, his wrists forever blurred in the midst of some strapping drive, or audacious reverse slap. He hit 103 off 137 balls, before Sarfaraz Ahmed and Misbah-ul-Haq took the reins – Misbah hitting the final runs in the gloom as fielders pleaded with the umpires that it was too dark to continue. Sri Lanka deserved to lose this match for their negativity, and the cricket gods dealt them justice. No matter, there would be victories to more than make up for this lapse in the months to come.

The story of Sri Lanka's World T20 campaign in March and April is worth a book in itself. Two days before the team set out to Bangladesh, Sri Lanka Cricket, who had by then made an annual exercise of entering a contracts dispute with their players, threatened to send a second-string team to the tournament if the players did not accept the pay cut the board proposed. In the end, an 11th hour compromise was reached, whereby the first-choice team would play in the World T20 without any active contracts.

After the team arrived in Bangladesh, the board and selectors had publicly played out spats with Kumar Sangakkara and Mahela Jayawardene, on top of which Dinesh Chandimal was removed as captain midway through the tournament for underperforming. This should obviously be a recipe for catastrophe, right? I mean, how can a team publicly at war with their board, and who have just sacked their captain ahead of the knockouts in a world tournament, be expected to perform? They looked as if they were about to crash out too, when they made only 119 batting first against New Zealand. Then Rangana Herath – who had not been picked in the XI until then – produced the greatest T20 spell ever, taking five wickets for three runs. Sri Lanka eased through the rest of the tournament, completely outwitting a red-hot India in the final. When they returned to the island, they found Colombo at the climax of a euphoric three-day party.

The most high-profile Test series of Sri Lanka's year was in England, and although it was just a two-match affair, those two weeks produced more theatre than most five-Test tours. There was Sangakkara's burning desire for a Lord's hundred in his last match at the venue. When he got to triple figures, lacing one of his bent-kneed drives through the covers, his great friend Jayawardene wrapped him up in a surprise bear hug. That would be one of their final century stands together, with Jayawardene announcing his retirement shortly after.

The last over of that first Test at Lord's was almost unbearably climactic. Sri Lanka, batting for a draw, had only two wickets in hand. Second delivery, Stuart Broad gets a short ball to hit Herath's glove on the way to the keeper, and the batsman walks without waiting for a decision. Only, the glove was off the bat handle when the ball struck it, and he should not have been out. England then thought they had won the match when No.11 batsman Nuwan Pradeep, who had basically headbutted the stumps trying to evade a bouncer in the first innings, was given out lbw. Broad and his teammates had raced out towards point,

as Lord's rejoiced around them. But Pradeep was certain he had hit the ball. He asked for a review and survived.

In the next match, at Headingley, it was England who were batting for a draw, after Mathews' spectacular 160 had helped overturn a 108-run first-innings deficit, and England's own No.11, James Anderson, was defending doggedly, denying Sri Lanka's bowlers for more than an hour. The penultimate ball of the match would prove his undoing, however. Eranga banged in a bouncer that Anderson lost sight of and, after taking the bat handle, the ball sailed to short-leg. Sri Lanka were ecstatic, racing to Eranga, piling on top of him, whooping like maniacs. An exhausted Anderson would later weep in front of the cameras as he accepted his award for Player of the Series.

Back at home, Sri Lanka faltered in a Test in Galle against South Africa, as Steyn delivered two blistering spells of violent reverse-swing, albeit perhaps aided on the first occasion by Vernon Philander's picking of the seam (he pleaded guilty to a tampering offence). However, it was the next series, against Pakistan, that produced the most unforgettable finish in a year of unforgettable Test finishes. Sri Lanka had brought another dead Test to life on the fifth day. Although the first innings of the game had only come to a conclusion in the dying stages of the fourth day, Herath rubbed his bowling defibrillators together and precipitated a Pakistan collapse on the fifth morning, leaving Sri Lanka 99 to win and less than 20 overs to get them in.

It appeared as if the hosts were going to get there, when almost out of nowhere, a monstrous, black cumulonimbus materialised, threatening to unleash its torrents at any moment. Just as suddenly the ground filled with spectators, trishaw drivers, street vendors and school teachers who had heard that the Test was hurtling to a juicy conclusion. Those who couldn't get into the stadium went up to the Galle Fort ramparts overlooking the ground – the best free view in all the game. Are you getting the picture? The grass banks are overflowing. The ramparts – an expanse of about 800 metres – are absolutely swarming. Mathews is at the crease, trying to bludgeon every ball into the nearby Indian Ocean, which has come to frothy, heaving life. The cloud over the stadium looks positively apocalyptic by now, but somehow it withholds its payload, and only as Mathews is playing the winning shot does the torrent come. By the time the batsmen have completed the run, they are soaked. So are the jubilant thousands who have come.

Looking back, it seems ludicrous that all of this could have unfolded over a mere eight months. That one team could be at the heart of so much chest-thumping, breathtaking fun. Sri Lankan cricket is never not unusual, but January to August 2014 went way beyond that. It was bloody insane.

Andrew Fidel Fernando is *ESPNcricinfo*'s Sri Lanka correspondent. His most recent book is *Upon a Sleepless Isle: Travels in Sri Lanka by Bus, Cycle and Trishaw.*

MELINDA FARRELL

2014/15

OUT OF THE DARKNESS AND INTO THE LIGHT

The gravest tragedy of cricket's century saw the game come together in sorrow and grief

I t began and ended in tragedy, but the spaces between were glorious; filled with friendship, joy and adventure. And cricket, of course. Rather a lot of it.

It started in November 2014, with a week in Bengaluru and the usual nightmare of frequent travel – I'd arrived but my luggage hadn't. Not until the day before my return to Australia, anyway. I had just joined *ESPNcricinfo* and was meeting many of my new colleagues for the first time as we formulated a plan for tackling a colossal few months, starting with a Test series between Australia and India, and culminating in the 2015 Men's World Cup.

A few months earlier, relatively broke and dissatisfied with the freelance television presenting work I was doing in Sydney, I rolled the dice on a trip to England. I knew Sambit Bal,

ESPNcricinfo's editor, was going to be at The Oval on day three of the fourth Test between England and India. I'd relentlessly hassled the poor man about work opportunities via email without success and I figured that if I was standing in front of him he simply couldn't avoid me. After scraping together every bit of work I could to pay for the airfare and accommodation, I cornered Sambit in the press-box overflow area as we watched England demolish India by an innings. Within 48 hours, I had a contract.

I arrived at the Bengaluru office in the cotton trousers I had worn since leaving Sydney and a donated ESPN t-shirt to hear the news of Phillip Hughes' death, struck by a ball in a shocking moment that devastated the whole cricketing community. I hadn't known him well but he was friendly and open and would often happily stop and chat where others might walk by. I looked at the bats placed outside in the corridors and tried to comprehend what had happened. I was asked to write a script but it took an age to record because I couldn't stop my voice shaking.

Back in Australia, my first assignment was Hughes' funeral in the country town of Macksville. It was a strange and unsettling experience, standing with other crews and filming the friends, family and cricketers as they walked down to the church. Other camera operators kept asking me to identify players and I felt the pressure of a new employee needing to make a good impression, and that meant getting the right shots. At the same time, I hated being part of the intrusion into the grief, while also grieving in my own small way. Emotionally, it was the most difficult day of my reporting career.

My most vivid memory of the first Test between Australia and India, which took place in Adelaide six days after the funeral, occurred late on the final evening, long after all the fans and nearly all the journalists had left. Sitting in the press box, I noticed the Australian players wander out, beers in hand, and gather around Hughes' Test cap number 408, painted large on the outfield. I realised they were about to sing the team victory song in his honour. I grabbed my camera and, in defiance of every health-and-safety regulation, knelt on the front desk and precariously leant out of the open window. It was a small camera with a modest zoom and I held my breath and tried to steady myself as the singing echoed around the dark, empty stadium. I woke up the next morning to see that my wonky footage was being broadcast all around the world.

My new job was exhilarating but challenging. I was a one-woman crew, setting up the camera and mics, dealing with technical issues, presenting, interviewing and feeding the footage for editing and publication. It was a new position and we had the freedom to try things and see what worked. My colleague Jarrod Kimber roped me into appearing on *Polite Enquiries*, talking smack about the day's play, laughing constantly, no second takes, loose as hell – and it was *work*. There were more serious chats with Ian Chappell, Rahul Dravid and Mark Nicholas, vox pops with fans, player interviews. I couldn't believe my luck.

The summer changed tempo with an ODI tri-series involving Australia, India and England leading into the main event. I began the World Cup in Christchurch for the tournament opener between New Zealand and Sri Lanka and then jumped back to Adelaide the following day for my first India v Pakistan experience. Adelaide sunsets are particularly vivid and, when combined with the cacophony of those two sets of fans, sitting in the stands was an extraordinary sensory experience. Throughout the tournament, I tried to add a sense of colour and fun to our coverage.

Jarrod, Abhishek Purohit and I raced each other around an obstacle course on Segways in Perth. George Dobell and I were ferried on three-wheeled motorbikes along the east coast of New South Wales after a visit to the Bradman Museum in Bowral. A pelican provided a *Polite Enquiries* highlight when, perfectly framed between George and I, it visibly shat during George's rant about England's performance. Such are the perils of self-shooting. I've had stray bra straps slip into view and even accidently up-skirted myself, although my worst wardrobe malfunction – splitting my pants on camera while trying to jump a fence to join a game of gully cricket in Chandigarh – did happen with someone else behind the camera.

During the World Cup I lugged around 45kg of luggage, most of it camera gear and transmission equipment. George described me as a human manifestation of the donkey in the game *Buckaroo*, while BBC commentator Daniel Norcross has told me a sure sign of summer's approach is my first appearance, carting what looks like my life's belongings along to a training session.

Those camera bags rode with me as the summer rolled on, the turning of autumn leaves heralding a change of hemisphere. To England, where the media pack immediately and generously accepted me as one of their own, and where I experienced my first Test match at Lord's. To India, where I slept in a tent at the foot of the Himalayas, learned to cook *dosa* and stood pitch-side as Carlos Brathwaite led West Indies to a "remember-the-name" World T20 victory. To New Zealand, where Brendon McCullum signed off from Test cricket with an outrageous 54-ball century in front of resilient Christchurch fans. To Malahide, and sipping a seaside pint after watching Ireland make their Test debut. To the Caribbean, where I played dominoes on the street with locals in Georgetown and saw Australia's women triumph in the 2018 T20 World Cup. And on and on, never tiring of the game and always learning new ways to love it.

My extended golden summer was only brought to a halt after Australia Women's next T20 World Cup victory early in 2020. As the pandemic took hold, I experienced my first full winter at home for more than six years, staying with my mother in rural New South Wales. I missed the people as much as the cricket: the friendships and kindness of colleagues providing the warmth of summer as much as the sun. But that yearning only deepened my appreciation. With any luck, some time in the future I'd be back again at a cricket ground, bags in hand, knowing that summer had finally returned.

Melinda Farrell is a freelance cricket journalist and TV presenter.

The Australian team sing their victory song in honour of Phillip Hughes

HEATHER KNIGHT

2017

THE DAY EVERYTHING CHANGED

*Ever wondered what it's like
to lift a World Cup?*

The summer started badly for me. I'd had a niggly foot during our pre-season trip to Abu Dhabi and the scan came back with a bone in my foot lit up like a Christmas tree. Not good. All I heard on the phone to our physio was "stress fracture", at which point I checked out. My mind began to catastrophise. That's it. Dream over. I'd miss my one shot at lifting a World Cup on home soil.

Dragging me from my thoughts, our physio tried to reassure me. If all went well, we could still find a way to manage me through it; oh, and by the way, the moon boot and crutches are in the post.

The next month was torturous. I'm a pretty level person, but being injured can push any cricketer to the edge. Watching the girls going about their prep at Loughborough, hopping around the boundary

and spending my time in the gym on the 'arm bike' – a God-awful machine that tests your ability to withstand lactic acid in your triceps – wasn't my idea of fun. I had the biggest tournament of my life coming up and I couldn't prepare how I wanted to.

My foot began to heal, but as the injury clouds cleared, I had a bigger problem: I couldn't buy a run. I played in a few practice games and didn't pass 10. My footwork felt slow and my timing had deserted me. Everything felt wrong. I hit more and more balls in the nets but just couldn't get my timing back. What was going on? I'd felt in fine fettle all winter, but now I was falling down the slippery slope into poor form and starting to doubt myself.

Two weeks before the start of the World Cup, I was sent to play purely as a batter in a warm-up match for Loughborough Lightning against Sri Lanka. I inelegantly misjudged a straight off-break hitting middle stump. Second-ball duck, thanks for coming. I slipped a little deeper.

Heather Knight lifts the World Cup trophy at a sold-out Lord's

Outwardly, I tried to appear relaxed, the group was in such a positive space and we'd built such belief. Inwardly, stress levels were high. Was I losing my cool? Was the pressure getting to me? How am I going to score any runs in this tournament?

I arranged to meet our sports psychologist at the time, Mike Rotheram, in our hotel in Chesterfield. I'd been bottling it all up, even to the people closest to me. I had to talk it through with someone. I don't find it the easiest expressing my emotions, but I told him how I was feeling, about the pressure I was putting on myself and the worry about where my next runs were going to come from.

Getting it all out there helped. Mike reminded me when I'm at my best with the bat. He spoke about the calm energy I have, and how I'm always looking to score. We had a practice game the next day. I resolved to not worry about the outcome and focus on taking the game on.

After a streaky start, something clicked and I was back. Suddenly, batting felt natural again. I made it to three figures and felt a weight off my shoulders. There and then, I promised myself that whatever happened during the tournament, I had to give myself a break. I vowed to embrace everything that would be thrown at me. This was a once-in-a-lifetime chance; all the more reason to confront it in the manner I wanted to.

Our coach Mark Robinson bought the team a round of Mr Whippys from an ice cream van at the side of the ground and into the tournament we went.

It was a strange start, not least because the security staff at Derby wouldn't let us into the ground. The batters travelled in an early minibus and they were expecting a coach, so they assumed we were a bunch of fans in full kit! Our assistant coach Ali Maiden, the resident minibus DJ, was blaring out Baddiel & Skinner, which probably didn't help.

And we lost. We'd been a bit shellshocked by some aggressive strokeplay from Smriti Mandhana at the start of India's innings and we struggled to get their spinners away. I remember having a conversation with Robbo before going to speak to the girls. We agreed to keep things quite positive, we both knew we'd been a bit overawed by the occasion, but we decided it was best to brush past that and focus on the next game.

We got back on track with a big win against Pakistan at Leicester with both Nat Sciver and myself scoring our first ODI tons in the space of a few balls. That was special. We were into the tournament. Now we needed to get on a roll.

A few days later we won a close game against the Aussies. After that one I really thought we would win it. We had so many different people performing and winning those big moments in tight games, it meant our confidence as a team was sky high. The day had begun with Robbo dropping his trousers believing that he had a pair of training shorts on underneath, only to realise that they were non-existent and having to scramble around pulling them up! It must have been another of Robbo's psychological masterplans to defuse any tensions…

At certain moments it hit me that things were different now, that women's cricket was changing. One of those came after our penultimate group game against New Zealand where Tammy Beaumont and Nat scored brilliant hundreds and the 'Natmeg' – a shot that sends the ball between her legs – was born. Joe Root was doing an interview the next day and he was asked what he thought of it. As female cricketers we're often asked about the men's game; to see it the other way around felt significant.

The greater spotlight was something new for all of us. Leading into the summer, there were some massive billboards of the captains to promote the tournament, including one at my local tube station. I was mortified when I had to get the train into town – sunnies on every time. It wasn't something I was used to or comfortable with.

After winning our remaining games to top the group, we just had South Africa blocking our path to Lord's. There were a few nerves around before the semi and I tasked Katherine Brunt with the job of getting everyone to crack a smile. She's a big Eminem fan and had started doing the odd funny rap in training and calling herself Kathy B. So I asked her to rap in the huddle. It was hilarious, and had the desired effect on everyone as we ran onto the field, although I regretted it slightly as Katherine's adrenaline-fuelled first over wasn't her finest.

The conclusion to that match was the most tortuous feeling of my life. Sitting on the balcony, having swept a rank full toss straight to the fielder, I watched as our hopes hung on a tricky chase we were messing up. Sarah Taylor and Tammy were singing to try and ease the tension – I think it intensified mine – and Alex Hartley was asking everyone's opinion on whether or not to wear a thigh pad. Somehow Jenny Gunn and Anya Shrubsole held their nerve, and when Anya struck the winning boundary with two balls remaining, the balcony erupted. Our much-loved doctor Tham jumped up and fell down a set of stairs. Luckily no medical assistance was required.

And so to Lord's, July 23, 2017. The day our lives changed forever.

As I stood there about to sing the national anthem, leading my country on home soil at a World Cup final in front of a full house, I looked up to the big screen to see the face of Rachael Heyhoe Flint, who was no longer with us. I scanned the crowd to find Eileen Ash, 105 years young, who had earlier rung the Lord's bell. In those moments I felt the true enormity of the day. What depths of gratitude we owed the women who had fought for us to be there. Today was for them too.

We posted a slightly under-par 228 and things were looking bleak with India 191-3 in the chase. Look at those figures now and it's hard to fathom what happened next, but in the heat of battle it genuinely felt like we were always in the game. Every little decision, every conversation, all felt critical. In a weird way that made things easier: keep calm, give clarity and trust my bowlers. With the game slipping away I had a decision to make. Which of the big two of Shrubsole or Brunt do I bring back? I went with Anya, planning on giving her a couple of overs before going back to Katherine. First ball: four. Second ball: four. Bugger. But Anya had a steely look in her eyes. A few balls later she picked up the key wicket of the set Punam Raut. I didn't need to say much, just keep her going and see what happens…

What followed was the best spell I've ever seen, as she charged through that Indian tail and wrestled the game back for us. Despite one of the most dramatic, dropped dollies in the history of the game when they were nine down, Anya was good enough to nail that final wicket with her very next ball. The elation in that moment was unlike anything I've ever felt and probably will ever feel again.

The moments in the dressing room afterwards are those that will stay with me the longest. Singing our team song and reminiscing with everyone on the balcony having achieved what we set out to do was unbelievably special.

As I looked out from that historic balcony, I thought how we'd cemented our spot in the game's history. There were the remnants of times gone past scattered throughout the day, even the old male member in the pavilion who sanctimoniously told me immediately after the toss, "You should have bowled first dear!". You could feel the ghosts of the women who had fought to bring us this chance. That day we walked in their footsteps, and it belonged to all of us. A new dawn, a new era. Women's cricket had arrived.

Heather Knight is captain of England Women.

Mark Wood lets it all out after a breathless finish to the World Cup final

MARK WOOD

2019

ACROSS THE UNIVERSE

In the 44-year history of the Men's World Cup, England had never won it. Something had to give.

I t all started for me in St Lucia. I felt that my Test career had stood still in 2018, and I wasn't fulfilling the potential people saw in me. That winter I lengthened my run-up and the change felt good, I felt more fluid, but I still hadn't been picked in the original tour party, and it was only when Olly Stone was injured that I got the nod. When I arrived, the coach Trevor Bayliss took me to one side and said he wanted to see a bit more 'mongrel' in me – that wasn't an Ashington word but I knew what he meant. I started to ramp it up in the nets, bowling as hostile as possible, hoping that attitude would feed into my bowling on the pitch.

I loved the whole atmosphere of St Lucia and felt very relaxed before that game, hoping I might get a chance but not expecting anything. I hadn't played a Test match since early 2018, so I wasn't

in that inner circle, yet I didn't feel entirely out of it either. I knew I was bowling well in the nets, showing some of that mongrel that Trevor asked for.

I was lying on a hammock in the hotel, just day-dreaming, enjoying the Caribbean air and the relaxed vibe, when I got a WhatsApp message from Rooty asking me if we could have a quick chat. At that point I thought I might be in, but you're still on edge for those minutes. He found me in my hammock and walked over, sat down and said, "You're in tomorra". And then those feelings of excitement, and then that wave of 'Oh no'. I'd be going back into the arena, having to prove myself yet again. And yet somehow it felt different this time. I promised myself I was just going to enjoy it. I was going to bowl as fast as I could.

We batted first, so I got to watch their bowlers. It was a nice stadium, with the grassy banks full of England supporters. When I was thrown the ball, I was put on at the end where the commentators were. Every time I walked back I could see Darren Gough and Steve Harmison, two of my idols. If I bowled a good ball I'd get the big thumbs-up from Harmy. It started coming out well. I got a taste for it. It was probably the first time in a Test match that Rooty could set any field and I wasn't paying any attention to it. All I could see was the batter and the stumps. In that spell every chink of the chain was there. I was so in the zone, I could let the ball fly.

Shimron Hetmyer's wicket was the one. He'd had a good series, and was the kind of player to get on the front foot and counter-attack, but he was tentative. It felt like a tick in my box that he was in his shell. By then I was flying, having already nicked off Shai Hope and then taken two in two, Darren Bravo and Roston Chase first ball. I still think about that hat-trick ball. Why didn't I just bowl at the stumps? He just left it! I'm still having to live with that. And I'll never forget Goughie's face of thunder in the commentary box…

I bowled eight or nine overs and I was knackered, so Rooty told me to have a break. Then we got them nine down and he called me to come back on. I said, "Nah, come on, it's embarrassing, you don't have to do that, it's about the team, let's just get it done and get off the field". Rooty wasn't having it. He told me that I was bowling the next over, and that was that. Looking back now, I'm so thankful to him for that. Getting that final wicket of Shannon Gabriel changed my career. Four wickets when you're bowling quick means you've done well. But to get that five-for, my first in Test cricket, it's a whole weight off your shoulders. You're viewed differently. And you feel different.

It was the first time I truly felt like I belonged. But there were bigger challenges on the horizon. Huge, terrifying challenges.

The days and weeks before the World Cup squad was announced were hellish. I didn't enjoy it at all. We knew that a superstar was coming in. Jofra Archer was going to take someone's place. Was it going to be him for me? Like for like, one 'fastie' for another? I'd done well in the West Indies on the one-day leg of the tour, so I knew I had a chance, but the wait was agony. I'll never forget the feeling when I got the call to say I was in.

Jofra blew us all away. Just watching him in those early days, the way our batters played him in the nets, you knew what we had in front of us. I bowled fast but they played me fine, and whacked me if I wasn't on it. But watching them play *him*, he was hitting them on the pads, the helmet, splaying their stumps. And all with a grin and a laugh. He's so laidback he could sleep on a washing line.

We were at home. We'd blitzed everyone for two years. If all went according to plan, no team would stop us. But you can write the story in your head, it never goes to script. In hindsight it makes a better story that we had to win our last four games – '*We came through the fire, and rose like a phoenix*' – but I can guarantee it didn't feel like that at the time.

The pitches weren't quite what we were used to, and we had a lot of games that came close together, but the facts were that after a winning start against South Africa, an early-tournament blip affected our confidence going into the Australia game at Lord's and after that one, we'd suddenly lost three games. The equation became grimly straightforward. One more defeat and we were out.

Before the India match, we sat down as a group to talk it through with David Young, our team psychologist. It was revealing to hear people like Stokes and Morgan – players that you'd think are bulletproof – talk about their vulnerabilities. Morgy's always calm, and Stokesy will never give up. He's a leader without being a captain. To hear these alpha males speak about their nerves and their fears, that really cut through to the rest of us, and made us connect to each other. It wasn't over the top 'lads stuff'; we didn't go around slapping each other on the back and talking about going over the trenches together; it was just a gentle, open, honest conversation. Our spirits were lifted.

And after that we were unstoppable.

Following the India win we headed up to Chester-le-Street to play New Zealand. My family and friends were all there; most of them won't travel 'beyond the wall', so this was the one they were all there for. I remember singing the national anthem with the England flag fluttering over Lumley Castle. That was special. And I bowled pretty well too.

I'd played every group game, and felt like I'd grown into the tournament. Having Jofra in the team brought out the best in me because I was trying to bowl faster than him. I'd bowl one delivery and it'd come up saying 88mph, and he'd be calling me 'Stevo', after Darren Stevens. So I'd try and push it and bowl my next ball as fast as I could, and it'd be short and wide and I'd get whacked for four, and he'd be there laughing at mid-off!

Australia, then. The World Cup semi-final. At Edgbaston. *This* is the ground you want to play them at. Lord's is nice, but it's very prim and proper, and the opposition always raise their game. Edgbaston has the *acoustics*. It's like a medieval fortress.

It was my 50th cap, and Stokesy said some nice things before the game, about how I'd stayed strong and resilient when times were tough. When David Warner hit the first ball for four, I feared the worst. We'd beaten them for two years straight, but this was the big one, and we'd lost to them in the group stage. *Surely* this can't happen.

After that first ball, Woakes was phenomenal, taking three cheap wickets. And Jofra was brilliant too, getting Aaron Finch first ball with one that was absolutely on the money. Our world-class leggie Adil Rashid then brought it home in the middle overs, and I got the last wicket, pulling this weird snarling face in the process. Trevor Bayliss saw it. "Finally," he said. "There's that mongrel we've been looking for…"

Lord's, July 14, 2019. We were there.

I don't get recognised much when I'm out and about. But that week in the build-up, it was happening everywhere. People were lining up to wish us good luck. That was how the mood in the country was at the time.

I actually felt strangely relaxed. It was only when a friend came down and we were having dinner that night in the hotel and he looked at me and said, "I can't actually believe that you're gonna play in a *World Cup final*" that I started to feel it again. The way he said it, in disbelief, just hit home. We used to play mini world cups at Ashington Cricket Club, him in his India shirt, me in my West Indies shirt. Now this. For real.

I hated the match. Absolutely hated it. I couldn't believe the way that I bowled in my first spell. I've watched it back since and been screaming at the telly. Why not just hit the top of off stump as hard as I can? I was too desperate to do well. I was in overdrive. It was only when I came back for my second spell and I got Ross Taylor out leg-before that I felt I was in the match. Suddenly I was in the battle with the *batsman*, not with that big sign that says WORLD CUP FINAL. I felt like I bowled well after that.

At the break Morgy said to us, "This is par, build partnerships and we'll win this". I trust everything the man says, so I sat back, fully confident, and put the flipflops on. That confidence lasted about 20 minutes.

It was so intense. Evenly matched, blow for blow, a fraught kind of game, and with what was at stake it became a terrible grind. I thought we'd lost it seven, eight, maybe a hundred times, all the while lurching from one extreme to another. I've never felt so sick knowing I might have to bat. I'm sitting there in my pads thinking that if Stokes gets out in this last over, I'll have to go in and hit a boundary. What was I going to do? I was actually close to throwing up. Morgy came up to me and said, calm as you like, "All good, boss?" "Yeah skipper, all good, no worries." Inside, I was screaming. When I went out to join Stokesy in that last over, I was wearing every conceivable bit of padding available to man. Little wonder I was yards short of beating the throw.

I wasn't even out there for the Super Over. I'd pulled a muscle in my side so I was on one of those old-school park benches by the side of the pitch, stood up. There was the physio, the doctor, the strength coach, and the lads who weren't playing. Moeen was giving ball-by-ball commentary. New Zealand need two to win off the last ball. I'm a mess. Jason Roy had mis-fielded earlier in the over. "We'll be alright," says Mo, "as long as the ball doesn't go to J-Roy…" He's always had great timing.

That night. Emotional, euphoric, togetherness, a bit of relief, a fair dollop of pride. We got back to the hotel, all of us still in our blue kits. Our families were all there. It didn't matter who it was, you'd be walking down the corridor high-fiving and hugging each other. I woke up with my medal still around my neck.

That morning we took the trophy to The Oval to meet some fans and schoolkids, and then on to Downing Street in the afternoon. On the Tuesday, when it came for us to go our separate ways, no one wanted to leave.

The days after were so strange. It was like a form of grief. You've won the World Cup and suddenly you're sat on your couch. It felt like I was waiting for something. Where was the next high, the next hit? It was like I'd lost something. We all felt it, this emptiness, this sense that we hadn't yet got it all out. In a funny way we still feel it now. Will it ever sink in? Do I ever want it to?

As the year rolled on, real life took over. My son was born in October, and I was there for it, the birth of my first child. And it led into the South Africa tour that winter, and a pretty useful one for me. As 2019 ticked over into the first weeks of 2020, I won my second Player of the Match award in a Test match, after St Lucia, for my nine wickets at Johannesburg. I felt I belonged.

Mark Wood is an England fast bowler, a World Cup winner, and the latest in an illustrious line of Ashington internationals.

SCYLD BERRY

2020

THE SEASON UNLIKE ANY OTHER

*The strangest summer
of them all*

As sunset approached at Old Trafford and the floodlights took effect, while Australia's batting collapsed in the third and decisive ODI, normally you would have expected 25,000 spectators – many well-lubricated – to have raised the roof with raucous songs about David Warner and Steve Smith. The sole sound, instead, came from the floodlights: nothing electrical amiss but the tweeting of hundreds of birds – swifts, martlets, house martins? – gathering to migrate and keeping themselves warm meanwhile by nestling on top of the lightbulbs.

This season has been my most memorable cricket summer. I have never felt so privileged to be covering the professional game, because almost nobody else could watch, and because I saw or sensed so much afresh. Normally I would never have sat

on the top floor of the Old Trafford pavilion in a hospitality suite, but social distancing demanded that I should look across to the Pennines and listen to birdsong, such as many of us heard for the first time.

Never has it been so important to have a human activity which lasts all day for several days and which has no relevance whatever to the material world; to have a niche or nest we can inhabit, free of anxiety, for respite. Cricket can be derided as a complete waste of time; but precisely because it consumes so much time, the summer of 2020 was invaluable.

The Bob Willis Trophy made my season: I only watched the Tests on television as the ECB admitted one correspondent per newspaper to the bio-bubbles at Old Trafford and Southampton, and my colleague Nick Hoult had taken over as the *Telegraph* cricket correspondent. I managed to see all five rounds of the BWT in part and the final at Lord's. I visited nine grounds in all,

The picturesque ground at Arundel became Hampshire's temporary home from The Oval when a crowd of 2,500 was admitted for Surrey's T20 against Hampshire, as a trial, to Grace Road when the whole of Leicester was locked down and bio-security was so strict that not even water was available, hot or cold. Overall I averaged 35.8, which would have been my highest batting average for many a season, except that it was my mean temperature when tested with a thermometer at the entrances.

It was weird going to the opening day of the BWT at Edgbaston on August 1, exactly one year after Stuart Broad had been roared on by the Hollies Stand in the opening Ashes Test. Nobody in the stands, nobody in the press box half an hour before the start, no sustenance, or so we had been warned, other than tea and coffee, and this at Edgbaston, hitherto the capital of catering in British cricket. Slowly, being a cricket match, and Edgbaston, things warmed up: the game between Warwickshire and Northamptonshire started, with sanitisation breaks every six overs; a handful of people – half media officers – trickled into the box; talk and humour could not be banned; and at lunchtime a cardboard box with a hot meal was served that would have shamed many an airline.

For this opening day of the county season, 2,500 spectators were going to be admitted to both Edgbaston and The Oval, until the government said no, two days before. I still do not fully understand. Spectators could have been instructed to sit in separate households, in the open air, on alternate rows, and to make extra-long queues for loos. Surely the virus would have spread more slowly among a couple of thousand in a cricket ground than in pubs and jam-packed planes. Live-streaming of county games escalated, as one beneficial consequence of Covid, but there is nothing like meeting and talking to people – two metres apart.

This privilege added piquancy. As in war-time, you appreciate pleasures more when others can't. It was not only my job but social responsibility to convey to readers the happiness to be had at these cricket matches, and I did not have to feign it. In atmosphere these BWT matches were like club or village games played by professional cricketers who had to supply their own applause. There was a zone or inner ring for players and coaching staff, but at grounds other than Leicester (where a player who left the ground could not return on the same day to collect his kit), the parameters could be relaxed. I have

Essex and Somerset face-off at an empty Lord's in the Bob Willis Trophy final

never learnt so much about wobble-seam than when listening to Worcestershire's bowling coach Alan Richardson on the boundary edge at New Road.

My favourite day? Arundel, I suppose, except it was not even half a day, just a morning session, before it rained and the Castle ground's old-time drainage could not cope. Sir Alastair Cook resumed on his overnight 75, with a nightwatchman, before Dan Lawrence played strokes that had gone down well in Australia on the Lions tour the previous winter. I took a chair and sat beside the sightscreen, on the grassy bank at one end, and heard the rare acoustics of that amphitheatre. Again, it was like birdsong one had never heard before – larks ascending in place of planes descending – as the ball hitting Cook's bat made a far deeper sound.

Although it was Arundel, Sussex were not involved. It was Hampshire's base for the summer while England used their Ageas Bowl. And gradually I understood what it must have been like to have watched or played cricket on this same ground in August 1914 – a game, say, between the Duke of Norfolk's XI and Free Foresters. Players had forenames like Tom and Felix, or Alastair, who proceeded immaculately to his century. Hampshire's captain started the day's play with a leg-spinner (Mason Crane). Nothing so rowdy as shouts and cheers from teammates if a batsman hit a boundary: most county sides cheered, but only polite applause at Arundel. Several marquees; the rich green vista over the Arun and across the Weald; no crowd, because the world was intent on more important things; and yet the game went on, a tiny bubble of its own, soon to be burst.

When I attended Lord's for the BWT final, the Indian summer ended on the eve of the game, replaced by a biting wind from the north. The silent, empty Underground. A city more unreal than Eliot could have known. Even Lord's was unfamiliar. Everything was in place around the pavilion – the lawns in the Harris and Warner gardens mown and manicured, flower boxes behind the pavilion, piles of hats with ribboned bands stacked neatly in the closed MCC and Middlesex Shop – but nobody around, and the whole Nursery End sealed, keeping cricketers out. Girders clanged behind the new Compton and

Edrich, reversing vehicles beeped. Nothing disturbed Cook while he batted all day, until the sun set in the gap between the pavilion and Warner Stand.

I will treasure Cook's 172 because he was more rounded – less angular, less tense with patriotism, I suppose – than in any Test innings, and he cover-drove with a flourish of his wrists to sign off the stroke. He ran – sprinted a couple of times – between the wickets as if chasing his spring lambs. His low-burn intensity and stubbornness were something unchanging in a world that had completely changed.

The media centre being out of bounds, we were quartered in the Tavern Stand, looking out on the autumnal field in the face of that north wind.

For the field is full of shades as I near a shadowy coast

Some of the figures were more ghostly than Francis Thompson's shades: faceless figures in masks, anoraks, bobble-hats and gloves, who ran on every over with caps and sanitising fluids, or to collect the sweater of the man about to bowl, as umpires were not allowed to do what they have always done.

An air of impermanence was heightened by the red advertisement in front of the Grandstand promoting the Ruth Strauss Foundation, bless her. Around the ground were signs supporting Prostate Cancer UK, the charity chosen to commemorate the late Bob Willis.

And a ghostly batsman plays to the bowling of a ghost

…who might have been old Bob, 'Goose' himself, running in from the Nursery End, bouncing hair and batsmen, pumping knees and elbows.

Lord's used to be called Dark's, after James Dark, who bought the lease, developed the ground then sold it to MCC. Strange to think that in the course of the following two centuries, even in war-time, this ground had never before seen so little cricket and so few cricketers as it did this summer.

Let us hope the new Dark Age does not endure.

Scyld Berry is chief cricket writer for the *Telegraph* and a former *Wisden* editor. His most recent book is *Cricket: The Game of Life*.